HIGHLAND HARVEST

A BARRA PONY

Copyright : Robert M. Adam, Edinburgh]

[Frontispiece

Highland Harvest

T. RATCLIFFE BARNETT

JAMES CLARKE & CO., LTD.
5 WARDROBE PLACE, LONDON, E.C.4

ACKNOWLEDGMENT

The majority of these chapters have appeared in *The Scotsman*; four have appeared in the S.M.T. Magazine; and one in *Scottish Country Life*. To the editors of these papers I am most grateful for permission to reprint the articles.

T. Ratcliffe Barnett.

MADE AND PRINTED IN GREAT BRITAIN BY PURNELL AND SONS, LTD.
PAULTON (SOMERSET) AND LONDON

1.

I've reaped fine harvests of beauty
  From the islands and bens and seas ;
Rich are the gleanings of mem'ry
  When I dream of the Hebrides.

2.

The wind vexed isles where I've wandered,
  With their machairs and golden sands ;
The clachans where many a welcome
  Was given with outstretched hands.

3.

Billows and breeze and spindrift ;
  A brown boat thrashing the ides ;
Flinging foam from her forefoot,
  And hissing seas from her sides.

4.

From many a lonely hilltop
  I've gazed with delight of yore ;
From Lui to Scuir nan Gillian,
  From Vorlich to far Ben More.

5.

Looking at sea lochs and islands
  On the map of God far below ;
Mid the ringing silence of summer ;
  In the dawn or the afterglow.

6.

Eagles soaring to heaven.
  In a giddy spiral of flight ;
Red deer crossing the balloch
  In the hush of a lambent night.

7.

The sound of voices now silent,
  By many a humble fire ;
Where the winds are drugged with peat reek
  When the ebbing tides retire.

8.

Blest be the faces remembered ;
  Blest be the voices now still ;
They make fine harvests in mem'ry
  Of a love which nothing can kill.

T. R. B.

24th March,
  1937.

CONTENTS

CONTENTS

ILLUSTRATIONS

I

ERISKAY: THE ISLAND OF SONG

ERISKAY was a great discovery—that little music-haunted isle which lies in the Atlantic at the southern end of the Outer Isles between South Uist and Barra. A telegram is sent to Eriskay from Boisdale for the motor boat, then an eight miles drive to Pollachar, and by the time the car arrives at the lonely inn of Pollachar the strongly-built ferry is waiting to take us over the four miles of shining sea to the Isle of Song.

The day was calm and warm, and the Atlantic was asleep. It is not always so, for the next time we went to Eriskay the Atlantic was racing through the sound like a sea hound unleashed. The hills of Barra rose from the sea on the south, with the isles of Lingay and Fuday floating in the ocean, and little Fiaray off the point of Scurrival.

We chugged into the harbour at Haun on the north side of the island, and set first foot on Eriskay with great expectations, which were not disappointed. The island is three miles long by about one across, with a considerable hill, Ben

Scrien, which rises from the centre of the island to a height of 609 feet. A little fleet of blue painted fishing skiffs lay in the harbour, and a glance at the names of the Boisdale and Eriskay herring boats shows that this is a world in which the Roman Faith still reigns supreme : The *Virgin*, *Immaculata*, *Mystical Rose*, *St. Bride*, *St. Joseph*, *St. Andrew*, and the like. In this far-away world every boat is blessed.

The first thing that made us feel that we were in a strange island was the sight of a little Barra pony picking its steps up the rocks, with great wicker creels slung on either flank to carry peats and merchandise. For there are no roads on Eriskay, only little pony tracks, and beaten paths among the grass. There is not a single wheel on the island, not even a wheelbarrow. Everything is carried on Barra ponies, and these sturdy little horses, with great rounded bellies and neat, well-bred legs, are led about by men, women, and children. They are so sure-footed that they climb the narrow paths and rocky hills with an unerring confidence. The very best paths, hard-beaten and stony, are only about five feet wide.

Thanks to the Government building subsidy, the houses are now well-built and comfortable looking ; but on either side of the island there are

still some of the old black houses, with the peat
fire in the middle of the floor, and the blue reek
coming out of door and windows. The people are
all well-conditioned, and the children are very
shy. One little boy was leading a pony, but when
he saw us he dropped the halter and took to his
heels, hiding himself in a tiny byre. There are
five hundred people in Eriskay, and all are Roman
Catholics except one man—a Skye man who keeps
the store. One hundred pupils attend the school,
and there is one family of fifteen on the island.
Indeed, the school has just had another large class-
room added to it.

The chapel of St. Michael and the Presbytery
are built on the very top of a rocky hill overlooking
the sea, and when the people go to Mass they have
to climb up mere footpaths among the flat rocks,
and all the turf on this hill of Zion is covered with
wild flowers. The chapel itself is a beautiful little
building, both outside and within, spotlessly clean,
with exceptionally tasteful Stations of the Cross,
and a chaste apse and altar. The silence within
was so intense and the restfulness so complete,
that it seemed natural to pray. When will all
our Presbyterian churches on the mainland and
in the isles learn this lesson of the ever open
door ?

The priest's handy man was cutting grass and weeding the walks. When I spoke to him he turned with the natural shyness of an Eriskay child, and went away to bring the priest's sister. He was so happy-looking that I asked if he was a bachelor, which hit the mark, and he smiled more than ever. On one occasion he saw some visitors bathing on the silver sands. After their dip they began to do some physical exercises, one of which entailed bending again and again with outstretched hands to touch their toes. It was high noon on a sunny day, and he exclaimed in horror : " They will be sun-worshippers ! " Having met the priest on the shore at Pollachar, I asked him if he often went across to Boisdale. With a twinkle in his eye, he replied : " Very seldom. You see, Boisdale is such an out-of-the-way place."

We all parted with laughter, for Eriskay is a happy isle.

Needless to say, I made my way at once to *Coilleag a Phrionnsa*, or the Prince's Strand. For, on this long sweep of heavenly white sand Prince Charles Edward Stuart landed from the *Doutelle* on July 23, 1745, to make his romantic bid for the throne of Britain. A little, bare-footed girl took me down the hillside and pointed out the rocks, half-way along the sand, where the royal landing took place. Alas for the cause, the Prince stumbled on the rocks when he stepped ashore. This was taken as an unhappy omen by those who were standing by. Here stepped ashore one of the most charming of the Stuarts, whose personality was so magnetic that he was able to persuade many of the chiefs almost against their will, certainly against their better judgment, to support him in his great gamble for a crown. Alexander Macdonald of Boisdale, Clanranald's brother, who had a house conveniently near at Kilbride, in South Uist, visited the Prince on Eriskay and refused to assist him, or to advise Clanranald to join him. He even implored Charles to return to France. But all in vain.

I picked some roots of the Prince's Flower which grows only on this spot. The tradition is that some seeds were scattered by the Prince himself, or fell from his ship's stores when the landing was made. I searched the many plants that were growing on the sandy grass, and found only one flower—a fleshy leaved, pink colvolvulus (*convolvulus major*). It was the very last bloom of the season, and it reminded me of the last flourish of the Jacobite Cause. Despite the popular legend that it grows only in Eriskay, it is known to grow elsewhere in Britain. Other flowers grow prodigal—blue milk-worts, wild borrage, orchis, silver weeds with their golden stars. Indeed, here as elsewhere on the Hebridean Isles, the yellow bedstraws and the flowers of the silver weeds make the machairs like a fairy carpet of gold.

The post office of Eriskay is a lowly thatched cottage, and the post master is a spry old man with a sharp face, clean shaven cheeks, a short grey beard on his chin, and a quaint fur cap on his head. He was dressed in the blue garb of a seaman, and he has that distinction of all great men—a mind of his own.

Eriskay is the island of incomparable Gaelic song, and to-day the world is singing some of those traditional airs which were found here by Mrs. Kennedy Fraser, whose dust now lies on the holy Isle of Iona. Coupled with her name must ever be that of Kenneth Macleod, the mystical sennachie who has discovered more about Celtic song than any other man alive. Indeed, he rediscovered the Road to the Isles, and his prose is of the order of the purest poetry, breathing the Gaelic spirit, both in sound and sense.

Above all, Eriskay is the isle that keeps calling you back. So we returned on a day when the sea

made the sound a pathway of yeasty foam. On
landing this time we made our way across the
island to *Acairseidh Mhor*, which means the Great
Harbour. From the hilltop we looked right out
to the Atlantic, between Barra with its gleaming
sands, and Pollachar, on the southmost tip of Uist.
But the eyes of the heart were continually drawn
down to the Rocks of Stumbling, and the wind
sang in the ears the sweet sad songs of a lost
romance.

It was a day of low lights, gleams of sunshine,
and flying showers. Passing over the hill, we
wandered down a little glen which leads to the
Great Harbour. Here it was windless and warm,
and men, women, and children were working at
the hay in the happy valley. They greeted us
cheerfully in the passing. How different this vale
of summer peace must be when the winter winds
drive the rain and mist for days on end over the
hill and down to the *Acairseidh Mhor* ! By the quiet
waters of this ideal harbour we sat and dreamed.
Two sunken rocks at the entrance made three sea
gates for the galleys of the sea kings long ago.
Voices kept whispering on the winds, and it
seemed as if at any moment a seal woman might
appear on the red wrack shore or a fairy wife on
the hill.

Then, rising up, we crossed the island again and embarked on the *St. Joseph*. The sea had risen, and we set out for Pollachar to battle against wind and wave, the salt spray drenching us all the way. But the *St. Joseph* had been blessed, and we made the voyage with peace in our hearts and this Gaelic old word in the mind :

> I see the hills, I see the strand,
> I see the host upon the wing,
> I see angels on the waves,
> Coming with speech and friendship to us.

II

UIST AND BENBECULA : THE WIND VEXED ISLES

THERE are two Uists, the North Isle and the South Isle, and between them lies Benbecula.

These islands are vexed in winter time with perpetual Atlantic gales which roar over the machairs and the hills. Even in summer time strangers who come to see their beauties are wearied by the weeping rains and the mists that hide the face of Heckla and Ben Mhor. But, how often I have seen them on the celestial days, when the sky was clear from rim to rim, and the sun shone out when the winds had fallen. Then indeed the peace of heaven seemed to brood over the little townships and the rolling moors.

Wherever you look there is beauty. Eastward from Boisdale, Rhum lies on the rim of the sea like a blue-grey cloud, framed between the rocky bluff of Ben Choinnich and the point of Calvey Island —Rhum, that altar isle of the sea, with a white cloud of incense rising from the twin peaks of Haskeval and Haleval. Westward, beyond the crofts of Daliburgh, lie the great machair lands, stretching green and flat, and always edged with the golden sands, which run for twenty miles, from Pollachar to Ardvachar. To-day, the machair is covered with shining silver weeds, yellow bedstraws, blue milkwort, swathes of golden ragwort, and a wealth of green thalictrum. What must the carpet of the machair be like a month earlier when the wild flowers are all in bloom! Away on the south rise the dim, blue hills of Barra, and all the isles folk who live in the croft houses of this seaboard are born and brought up on the sound of the infinite ocean which is forever thundering at their doors.

In this paradise of sunlight and colour the wine winds seem to drug the people into a drowsy lethargy which slows down the very clocks and makes the busiest feel that there is always plenty of time.

Numberless freshwater lochs gleam in the boglands, like turquoise eyes of earth which borrow their colour from the heavens they are forever beholding. The crofters' houses stand conspicuous and secure on their green knolls or on the long level horizons. Never have I seen so many waterlily lochs, on which to-day there must be tens of thousands of blooms. In Benbecula and South

LOCH BOISDALE AND SOUTH UIST

[To face page 20

Uist the beauty of these fairy cups of pearl and
gold is indescribable. I was constantly reminded
of a saying of Mahomet :—" If you have two loaves,
sell one and buy lilies, for bread feeds the body,
but lilies nourish the soul." In these islands I saw
no sign of grinding poverty. Men, women, and
little children, by their words and faces, testify to
a happy content. For the Hebrid Isles which lie
furthest south are full of music, song, and the
dance. I saw no Celtic gloom.

At Milton we loitered over the site of Flora
Macdonald's home. Standing by the rickle of
stones and grass-grown founds, I took off my
blue bonnet at the mere recollection of that brave
and cultured lady who, with a rare inventiveness,
bluffed the red coats, and at all risks to herself
took Prince Charlie across to Skye dressed as
" Betty Burke," her clumsy serving woman. It
seems a pity that there is no kind of direction or
memorial on the spot to guide the passer-by to
the site of old Milton House.

At Pollachar, which is at the southmost tip of
the island, the Atlantic glittered in the sunshine,
and over yonder is the little isle of Eriskay, the
home of Celtic song and story. Above the rocks
at Pollachar stands a solitary pillar of stone on a
green knoll, the silent memorial of those sad old

days when Druids celebrated their barbarous rites long ere the Christian missionaries came to the isles with the Good News.

Ancient tradition constantly jostles modern custom in the Hebrides. Let me give but one example. There is an old thatched cottage not far from Boisdale, where, nearly forty years ago, I had a strange experience. We went in to ask for a glass of milk. A comely mother was sitting at her spinning wheel, with her little girl beside her, and an older girl close by. There was plenty of peat reek and no English then in many of the black houses. Not wishing to offend the Highland woman by paying for the milk, I offered a silver coin to the little girl. In her shyness she ran to her mother's knee and hid her face in her broad lap. The woman then spoke in Gaelic to the older girl, who immediately went over to the kitchen dresser and handed down a broken mirror. Raising the face of the little girl, the mother made her look into the mirror. Strange to say the charm worked, and the child came for the offered coin. From very ancient times the mirror has stood for Wisdom, the magic of Reflection, and the Mystic Power that lies behind it. Symbolic mirrors are carved on many of the old Celtic stones. But the sequel to this story completes the interest of it.

For, on returning to Edinburgh that summer, I repeated the tale to a lady who had just returned from Eastern travel. Without a comment, she took me over to a corner of her room where stood the model of a Shintu Temple which she had brought home from China. And there, in a shrine similar to the monstrance in which the sacred Host is kept in Roman Catholic churches, she showed me a tiny bit of mirror.

From end to end of the Outer Isles you will find the ruins or sites of numberless duns—those primitive fortresses of the early inhabitants of the Isles. Old cells or chapels of the saints. Underground houses, where the wee folks were supposed to live. Standing stones on the lonely moors. Windswept graveyards on islets or promontories. Here there are relics enough to employ months of leisured research for those who have the mind and time. Occasionally in some of these God's acres you will come across a beautifully carved slab. There is one such resting place on the dunes beyond Daliburgh, sheltered from the Atlantic gales by walls and the natural slope of the ground eastward. There is a fine view inland towards Loch Hallan. The graves are mostly modern. But, near the foot of this great enclosure, there is a knoll which looks like the site of an old

chapel. Just here, among the long grass, I came
upon a typical Celtic slab with the remains of
beautiful carving on it. Having laid bare this
ancient memorial, I sat down and dreamed of the
far off days when the finest of the arts was cultivated by the Celtic monks in these Outer Isles.
The blue waters of Loch Hallan, with an edging
of yellow ragwort; the green machairs; the golden
sands; the restless ocean with the never-ending
sound of breakers on the shore; winds invisible
blowing across the graves—what a poem of life
and death in a setting of abiding beauty!

The abiding beauty reminds me of the Celtic
view of death. When a woman of the isles weeps
for anyone who has been drowned, it is said that
her tears fall in drops of blood on the heart of
her beloved, in that Land under Waves, *Tir-fo-
thuinn*, where the drowned one waits the coming
of the White Ship with the golden rudder, the
silver masts, and the silken sails, which is to bear
him back to *Tir-nam-beo*, the Land of the Living.
But a *bodach*, or old man, spoke wise comfort when
he said of the weeping woman—" It is a sad thing
that a woman should be drowning her husband
a second time with the tears she will be shedding."
There was another woman of the Isles who, being
bereaved of her daughter, wept bitter tears. But

she, too, had seen something of the beauty that
lies beyond the hills of home. So, looking up
into the face of her comforter, she said with a
smile that was like a rainbow shining through a
shower, " Why should I be sitting here crying
for Mary, when she has just slipped over the
beallach before me, and I will soon be following
her ? "

Woe to those strangers who come to the Isles
and can see nothing but rain-swept machairs,
melancholy seas, and gloom in the hearts of the
people. As the seas can laugh with a glittering
joy as well as moan with a death croon, so can the
Isles Folk be as merry as the sunlight at a *ceilidh*,
though they be sometimes as sad as a day when
the mist is down on the sodden moors. They are
makers of music as well as children of tempest.
But to those who keep harping on about the Celtic
Gloom, be it said at once, that all such travellers
bring gloom in the luggage of their own souls.

We left the Isles in the small hours, when the
witchery of night was on the sea, having received
the hundred thousand welcomes, and that hospitality which comes from the heart. We found
music, song, and story among a people whose
elemental simplicities are as yet unspoiled by the
ruder ways of a world that is very far off.

c

"Bright are the golden and green fields to me,
  Here in the lowlands ;
Sweet sings the mavis in the thorn-tree,
  Snowy with fragrance :
But, oh for a breath of the great North Sea,
  Girdling the mountains !

Many a hearth round that friendly shore
  Giveth warm welcome ;
Charms still are there as in days of yore,
  More than of mountains ;
But hearths and faces are seen no more,"
  Once of the brightest.

III

FORDS OF THE HEBRIDES : THEIR BLAZING BEAUTIES

THERE is no part of the Highlands which can be compared to the Fords of the Outer Isles.

We set out from Boisdale on a heavenly morning of blue skies and white clouds, summer heat, and fine visibility. In an August of broken weather this was the day of days. So we seized it. Motoring northward towards Carnan, on the South Uist side of the first Ford, we passed through the long flats of the Atlantic seaboard, which is all green machair, brown bogland, riddled with fresh-water lochs, and many crofting townships. The roads of South Uist are flat and well kept, with no hills or gravel washouts. The road at one point cuts across the waters of Loch Bee on a beautifully-built causeway.

When we reached Carnan Inn we found an old-fashioned wagonette with two horses waiting for us, all such appointments being made in the islands by telegraphic communication. In this wagonette we were to do the whole day's journey : first across

the South Ford, which is one mile; then across
the six miles of Benbecula by road; across the
North Ford, which is three and a half miles, to
North Uist; and back the same way to Creagorry
—the best part of twenty miles in a wagonette,
at a jog-trot, or a leisurely walk, with many a
splash through sea water, which more than once
came up to the horses' knees. The sun blazed
down all the way and burned face and knees as
red as beetroot.

The South Ford, which lies between South Uist
and Benbecula, is an open mile of sand at low tide,
and at full tide a shallow strait of the most beautiful blue-green sea water. It is easy and straight-
forward, and the horses knew their job. Benbecula, which looks so flat and uninteresting from the
sea when you sail down the east coast in drenching
rain and stormy weather, is a land of great beauty
on the west side. Indeed, it has all the glamour
of a Holland landscape—an enormous sweep of
sky, white clouds hanging in the blue, and infinite
vistas reminding one of old Omar's striking ex-
pression:

"That inverted bowl we call the sky."

Far to the north over this painter's palette of
many colours rise those blue sentinels, Eaval and
Burrival, and just as far to the south the great

massive of Heckla and Ben More. So, Benbecula lies between the Uists, cut off by the North
and South Fords, a lonely little world of its own
with its one rounded hill of Rueval. We passed
many tinkers' tents by the roadside. These are
generally pitched most cunningly by the side of
a good trout loch with a peat stack close by. For
tinkers' morals are easy when it comes to fish or
a fire, and nobody in these islands grudges them
their perquisites. A wedge of wild geese flew
above us. White swans with their little cygnets
floated on the blue waters of a loch. The air
was drenched with peat reek. Far out over the
Atlantic the Monach Isles floated in the haze,
and on clear days the stacks of St. Kilda rise like
needles out of the sea. Turn your eyes eastward
and you will see the distant headlands of Skye.
There are many Barra ponies on the island. We
passed a white one which was said to be thirty
years old, and it was still doing light work.

But, here we are at Gramisdale, and the horses
begin the long journey over the three and a half
miles of sand between Benbecula and North Uist.
In the pools and channels left by the receding tide
women were spearing flounders, altogether
oblivious of the discomfort of walking through
the pools with their skirts seeping in the water.

As the horses trot and amble on it seems as if these
great sands had been gleaming in the sunshine for
ever, with countless little rocky islets rising out of
them.   Then, a stream of water lying east and west,
and the horses splash through it.   We are now
nearly at the centre of the Ford.   Yonder to the
right is Grimsay ; to the left, Trialabreck and
Sunamul ; and in front a line of rocky islets which
make the backbone of the Ford—Eilean Iocrach,
Caigionn, Eilean na h'Airidh, and Eilean Mhor.
The way lies through this backbone of islands
between Caigionn and Eilean na h'Airidh.   Then
the track turns to the left, and after another mile or
so you are safely at Carinish in North Uist.

That is a mere word direction.   But no words
can ever describe the blazing beauties of these
Uist Fords on a summer day like this.   The infinite
sands, the islands rising out of the golden floor, the
dim blue mountains on the horizon, red wrack,
sapphire pools gleaming like jewels, runnels of sea-
green water, and a swirl of snowy clouds hanging
over the isles of dream.

If you miss the tide, you must make up your
mind to sit down on some island like Trialabreck,
which has a rocky escarpment at one end.   There
you must wait for hours, thanking God that you
have found such a safe refuge.   There is a small

cairn of stones at one part of the sands which commemorates the drowning of a man who was caught all alone by the waters at this spot when the flood tide set in. The Atlantic is merciless to a foolish loiterer.

But, having time to spare, we took our lunch on one of the little grassy islands towards the south side of the Ford. The patient horses waited on the sands, and we basked in the heat. It was with a sigh of regret that we rose to depart, for surely here, lying on the back, gazing round at the solitudes of sand, and up into the infinite blue of the sky, we had reached a sanctuary of silence where none could intrude.

Returning to Benbecula, we made our way once more at a jog-trot down the island. But, when we reached Creagorry, nothing would satisfy our generous hostess but that we should take her motor-car back to Gramisdale and see the whole eastern seaboard of the island.

At the bay of Calligeo, beyond Balivanish, we lingered over the view to the north. As far as the eye could reach the sand gleamed golden, sweeping north, mile upon mile, to be lost at last in the haze of distance.

There is fine farming land on the west of Benbecula. All round Nunton, which was once a famous farm, but now broken up into crofts, I saw fields of waving crops, many of them barley, such as I have never seen in any crofting district of the Highlands. The great stone pillars at the north and south entrances of Nunton, and the old house itself, tell of an ancient glory which has now departed.

This is a land of old Church memories, as Nunton plainly shows. Well might that sailor saint, Brendan, marvel at the glow of many a holy lamp as he voyaged northward :

> " He heard, across the howling seas,
>   Chime convent bells on wintry nights ;
> He saw, on spray-swept Hebrides,
>   Twinkle the monastery lights."

At Balivanish there are the remains of *Teampull Chaluim Cille ;* at Nunton there is another old Chapel ; and three miles farther on there is the considerable ruin of Borve Castle, with a *Teampull* close by. The local tradition is that there is an underground passage running from the Castle to the neighbouring knoll. On North Uist, not far from Carinish, there is a great God's Acre with the ruined Church of *Teampull Trionaid*, the Church of the Trinity. Truly these Outer Hebrides were the Islands of the Saints.

At the pier of Creagorry we found the motor-boat awaiting us, for now the South Ford was full, and we sailed back to South Uist. The water was blue-green, for this Ford is comparatively shallow. Between the sand below and the sunshine above it was one sheet of iridescent beauty.

But this is a timeless world out here. I suppose no two clocks register the same hour to a minute in these leisurely islands. The soft Atlantic climate seems to lull into drowsiness all who dwell in this lotus land of peace and floating lilies. But when it comes to the Fords, the men who drive or ride over these mighty floors of ocean know to a minute when to catch the tide, and are alert to every issue of life and death. A little stone we passed on the limitless sands was especially significant, for the driver said : " So long as the tide is not up to that stone it is safe to go on ; but, if the water has covered the stone it is time to turn back." Only those who have been born and bred on the shores of the Fords can take a certain amount of risk, and they have sometimes had to swim their horses and let the wise beasts seek their own way to safety.

IV

THE FLOORS OF HEAVEN: FLOWERY MACHAIRS AND GOLDEN SANDS

THE last time I visited the Fords of the Hebrides we had to stand at Carnan, on the north tip of South Uist, and wait, and wait, and wait. For in spite of the usual telegram sent from Lochboisdale for a trap to meet us and take us across the South Ford to Benbecula, no trap was waiting for us. Maclean was away in the fields. So we had to wire across to Creagorry, and wait once more. Again and again I took the field-glasses and searched the Ford, which is about a mile across. At long last, I saw an old dogcart entering from the Benbecula side, with two collie dogs gambolling in front. When the dogcart arrived we climbed in and just got over the Ford in time. Even so, the water was up to the belly of the horse, and the dogs had to swim. As we had to cross the Ford a little to the east from the ordinary route, we arrived after a nerve-shaking jolt over the rough places, but we forgot all the weariness of waiting when we received the never-failing welcome at

Creagorry. A car took us up the six miles or so of the island to the North Ford, which was now fast filling. It had been a day of many miscalculations. But the islesman has more sense of eternity than of time, and after all, there are occasions in life when clocks are mere absurdities. It all turned out for the best, for we made up our minds to laze about in the sunshine, and we got our reward, for we enjoyed a feast of beauty such as we never could have had if we had crossed the three miles of sand. Near to the old inn of Gramisdale we camped out on the sun-baked turf the livelong summer day.

It was indeed a day of heaven, with clouds and sunshine, blue skies, and a fresh wind blowing—just the conditions that make for brilliant light and fine visibility. The wind chased the clouds, the clouds cast great shadows on the sand, the shadows chased one another, and the colour of the Hebridean world was indescribable. The Fords that day were like the Floors of Heaven. And yet it is the eternal artist in a man that makes him ettle after painting the impossible, whether it be with brush or pen.

The Ford was now filling rapidly, and woe be to the man who in ignorance defies it. The only price for that foolishness is death. In the deeps and shallows of the sand the blue-white sky was reflected where the moving waters made mirrors of the glassy tide. When you are crossing back and forward between Benbecula and North Uist, your attention is taken up with all the details of the journey, including the wisdom of the old horse in the gig. But, lying here on the hot grass, hour after hour, gives you the chance of a lifetime to watch the birth of one beauty after another. The long line of North Uist was one wash of amethyst, and the white houses of Carinish stood gleaming on green fields where these met the sands. The grassy islands of Sunamul and Triala-breck were like emeralds set in gold.

I walked right out on to the sands to watch the tide coming in. Except for the hum of wind in the ears, there was no sound. Slowly, silently, like a thief, the water seeped in, with a terrible sense of the inevitable. Soon, every hollow of the sand was filled, so that the spot where I stood was always being surrounded, and I had to shift my ground. The mighty Atlantic was behind each trickle. But out yonder in the west the ocean was already flooding in, with its deep blue waves which no power on earth could hold back.

And yet the inventiveness of man can so man-œuvre the powers of Nature that he can often overcome them by setting one natural force against another. For when the channel was well filled, we suddenly saw the tops of two masts and the tips of two brown sails moving quickly behind the grassy promontory on which we sat. It was a large fishing boat making for the open sea through the fast-filling Ford. Soon she appeared from behind the promontory, and we saw that she had set a jib as well as the two brown lugs and was reaching close hauled against both wind and tide. Her speed in the circumstances, however, seemed absurd, until I heard the hum of her motor. Then, I realised that man no longer is at the mercy of one element like the wind or the tide, but that he can use several to overcome whichever one opposes him. We watched the brown-sailed boat racing like a spirit to seek the Atlantic, across miles of sand, which had now become miles of deep water.

Then we went up the path to explore the ruined inn of Gramisdale. It was once a wild and primitive place frequented by drovers and seamen. The walls are three feet thick, and, standing as it does on a green knoll on the very edge of the sands, it commands a wonderful view of the islands and the North Ford. What a place it must have been on a wild wet night, when the wind was shrieking like a storm fiend and the darkness was like a funeral pall! The old road still goes down to the Ford past the ruined inn, and the tall stone-built beacon stands on the rocky escarpment.

But the colour of the day was as yet only half revealed, for the Floors of Heaven are to be found, not only on the golden sands, but on the flowery machairs of the Hebrid Isles.

On the way back we took the road, as usual, down the west side of Benbecula, and at Balivanish climbed a little green hill to get a better view. All the silver and sapphire wonders of the Ford were still spread below us, gleaming in the sunlight. But the foreground of the picture was almost as wonderful as the horizon. Here, the great flats of Benbecula lie between you and the blue waters, field after field of yellow flowers, bedstraws, buttercups, and silver weeds, and I know not how many other blooms. Indeed, the miles upon miles of flowery machair land on which you can walk on this edge of the world are liker the Floors of Heaven than any other pleasaunce on which I have ever travelled. Beyond the flowers, ten or twelve miles of shining sand sweep away north-wards by Eachkamish, Baleshare, Kirkabost Island and far Balranald, a thin line of snowy surf breaking between the blue ocean and the golden sands. Three thousand miles beyond these tumbling waters lies the New World, which has drawn generation after generation of highland adventurers and reluctant emigrants, all of whom have the heart's memory that never forgets. Yonder are the Monach Isles or Heisker, a long flat island with an edging of sand lying, dim and elusive, in the lap of the eternal seas. The misty stacks of St. Kilda, too, where a nobleman, with a love for its myriad sea-birds, has prepared for himself a summer home.

But words must ever fail to give any idea of the colours on the Atlantic seaboard of the Outer Hebrides. Adjectives, which are the pitfalls of a word-painter, soon get used up. Distances are so great that you have always to be measuring the mileage of machair and sand on your ordnance sheet, lest you exaggerate. This at least is true, that there is no painter's palette in Scotland so prodigally splashed with colour as these magic Floors of Heaven.

V

THE ISLAND OF CANNA : ITS ANCIENT LORE

THE islands of Canna, Rhum, Eigg, and Muck form the unique Parish of Small Isles. Lying in the lap of the Little Minch, these four islands are more or less inaccessible to the ordinary tripper. Each is very unlike the other, and of the four Eigg and Canna have those delightful features lacking in most of the outer isles—green pastures and woodlands. When I think of Canna I think of the dawn. For I arrived from the Outer Isles at dawn, and on leaving I boarded the steamer at dawn.

Canna was one of Clanranald's islands. The first house of the chief is still standing on the shore near the Post Office. His second house was the low, white cottage, with flanking out-houses, on the shore in front of the present ivy-covered mansion-house. I was told that in the chief's time this house had three storeys in the centre, with a one-storey extension on either side. On looking up the " Statistical Account " (1796) I find this corroborated. At the beginning of the description of the Parish of Small Isles there is a quaint engraving of a drawing by Lieutenant John Piercie, Royal Navy, with the chief's three-storey house in the foreground; two long boats are being rowed ashore: and a couple of frigates are letting off their guns in the harbour. Clan-ranald sold the island to the McNeills, and McNeill then built the present mansion-house which stands in the midst of trees. The fourth House of Canna was built by the grandfather of the present pro-prietor. It stands on high ground above the present mansion, and commands a magnificent view. Apart from the crofters' houses on Sanday Isle, which is joined to Canna by a bridge, with one or two houses for shepherds and workers, there is no township on Canna. Most of the people are Roman Catholics, so there is a Roman Catholic chapel on Sanday, and a beautiful little memorial Parish Church built by the proprietor's family near the pier.

The scenery of Canna is varied. You can climb the heather hills, wander over moors, stand on beetling cliffs, walk among fields, sit among the fruits and flowers of gardens enclosed, or listen to the wind in the trees. If you leave the meadows and climb to the top of the highest hill (690 feet)

D

you will look upon a panorama of sea and land scarcely to be surpassed. In the west you see Barra, Eriskay, South Uist, Benbecula, and North Uist. Northwards Skye fills the horizon from Neist Point to the Point of Sleat. Eastwards lies the mainland from Knoydart to Ardnamurchan, with Rhum, Mull, Coll, and Tiree floating on the summer seas. Due south lies the rocky isle of Heisker, with the lighthouse which sends its powerful flash across nine miles of sea right into your bedroom window.

Like many of the lonely islands of the Hebrides, Canna is full of the remains of Celt and Viking, holy men and pagan worshippers. But to any visitor the two most prominent features dominating the harbour are the Compass Hill and the Castle of Coroghon. The Compass Hill is so full of iron ore that anyone standing on the top of it with a compass will find the compass varying to a quarter of its dial.

The Castle of Canna has a more romantic interest. It is built on the corner of Coroghon Mor, a square stack of conglomerate rock on the shore. A steep and rather dangerous path leads up the rock from the landward side to a little door in a building of at least two storeys. On the seaward side the rock has a sheer drop of 70 feet. On the flat top there is a hollow basin which may have been used as a quarry for building stone. There is another pit, in all probability used as a rain-water tank. No wonder that Pennant wrote : " This tower was built by some jealous regulus [chief] to confine a handsome wife in."

A local legend has it that the regulus was Clanranald himself. He had a long standing feud with Macleod of Dunvegan. Young Macleod on one occasion was storm-stayed on Canna, and while there fell in love with the Clanranald heiress. News of their love came to Clanranald in South Uist and he set sail for Canna. But young Macleod took flight when he saw the chief's galley approaching, and the father in anger shut up his daughter in the keep of Coroghon Mor. But that is never the end of a love story. One stormy night young Macleod returned to Canna. The storm had put the guards off their vigilance and he got below her window. There he began to sing a song his lady love knew well. Between the gusts of wind she heard him. With the old inventiveness of love she knotted her bed sheets together and escaped down the unguarded side of the rock. So they both escaped to happiness.

The antiquities of Canna fill an antiquary's heart with joy. The place called A Chill or Keils

is an undulating meadow fragrant with a fine crop
of hay. Here there was a Columban settlement
in the very early days of the Celtic Church. Be-
sides being the holy site of one of the Columban
Churches there are four other antiquarian remains
in this meadow. On the site of the original Church
there stands a most interesting old Celtic cross.
It is of weathered yellow sandstone, has originally
been about 8½ feet high, but is now reduced to
about 7 feet. One side arm has been broken off,
but what is left of the sculpturing is of great
interest. At the very top of the shaft there is an
animal with an elephant's head and trunk, the fore
legs of a horse, and rudimentary hind legs. Below
that, there is another animal turning back on itself
and biting its own body. Then comes a little
bag-shaped ornament above a horse on which a
man is riding. Still further down is a sculptured
representation of a *magus*, one of the Wise Men,
with a long beard. His right hand is outstretched,
and he is kneeling with a bag of gifts in his left
hand, before the Holy Mother who holds the Child
on her knee.

Further west across the field there is a fine
Standing Stone, highly polished in places and
apparently dressed. Still nearer the sea in the same
meadow is the local burial ground, against the

outer wall of which is a very old shaft broken across the middle. On the upper part there is a Latin cross incised. This may well be the oldest Christian relic on Canna. It is of a very early type, and was probably removed from the site of the Columban Church to its present place. Inside this graveyard, lying among the long grasses, is a mica schist slab with some interesting carving.

Along with these relics may here be mentioned the Serpent Stone. It was described to me twenty years ago by a lady whom I chanced to meet while travelling. She had been a regular visitor to the House of Canna, and at that time the stone stood on the lawn of the mansion-house. It stands now within the beautiful little Celtic Church on the pier road. I took a sketch of the one side and a rubbing of the other. It is quite evidently two fragments of a cross shaft fractured in the middle. Carved in low relief on one side is the lower part of a human figure clad in a tunic. The tunic is hemmed, and has on it a bit of Celtic interlacing. Round the legs a serpent writhes. The other side of the stone has two panels of Celtic ornament, the lower being a fine design of four serpents interlaced.

Another interesting relic took us a few miles westward along the shore towards Tarbert. Tarbert, of course, means the low and narrow neck of land between two seas, across which the Vikings were accustomed to drag their boats. Then we struck to the right across the hills to the Point of Langanuish. There, on a flat green machair above the sea, we found a very large oblong kerb of stones with an outer chamber. The burial cairn has evidently been despoiled long ago. But the kerb is of rather a rare type. There is one similar in Arran and another in Colonsay. In the Arran grave there were found bones, boat rivets, a coin of the ninth century, and an Anglo-Saxon styca (a coin of the smallest denomination in the Northumbrian coinage) of the time of Vigmund, Archbishop of York (A.D. 831–854). In the Colonsay burial-ground there were found parts of the skeletons of a man and a horse, boat rivets, and clinker nails, weapons and three stycas, one of which was of the reign of Eanred (A.D. 808–840), and another issued by the same Vigmund of York. So these burials may be dated as not earlier than the close of the first half of the ninth century. Sitting on the heather above the Viking's grave, I thought of the fair-haired rovers of the sea who ruled these islands for over 400 years. What seamen they must have been ! For their viking ships were but small affairs compared to the most modest of our ships to-day.

A little further inland on a mound covered with bracken, below the slope of Ben Tighe, we examined two underground earth houses. One of them we entered by dropping feet-first into the abyss. An imaginative man feels apprehensive of being caught about the knees by the Wee Folk who used to live there at some time or other before now. The entrance is little over 18 inches across. There is a very heavy lintel, and there are several recesses just big enough for a small man to recline on. These two houses are unusually small, and there may be others on the same green mound.

Still further west on the grassy terrace above the cliffs at Garrisdale Point, there is a standing stone 3 feet high. A circular hole is sunk in this stone $8\frac{1}{2}$ inches from the top. The hole itself is $1\frac{1}{2}$ inches in diameter and $2\frac{1}{2}$ inches deep. The legend is that this is a thumb hole. The culprit to be punished had to thrust his thumb into it, and wedges were driven in until the thumb was either crushed or destroyed. Hence the name— Stone of Punishment. The three lines radiating downwards from the circle are problematic.

The last place of antiquarian interest I shall mention is to be found between Tarbert and Garrisdale Point. It is an old Altar with a Well at *Sgor nam Ban Naomha*, or the Rock of the Holy Women.

It stands on an exposed green terrace on the pre-
cipitous south side of Canna, and is evidently
the remains of an ancient monastic settlement.   In
all probability it was a nunnery. The place is
exceptionally remote. Basaltic escarpments isolate
it on the landward side, and access from the sea
is possible only in fine weather. The enclosure
is about 40 yards in diameter, and the surrounding
dry stone wall has been five feet thick. Four
structures have been built against the wall, and three
others stand near the centre. There were doubtless others, and these may have been cells.

Two of the little buildings were very plainly
a well and a mill. In the well a spring rises in a
bason of masonry. The water runs in a channel,
dips down below the ground, and appears again
in the bottom of the mill-house, where it is joined
by another subterranean spring. This mill is
similar to the very ancient corn mill on Taransay,
Harris. In the upper part there is an aumbry.
A single chambered structure next the mill is D-
shaped. Within it is a circular platform with a
low rectangular erection which contains some
stone pounders and the fragment of a saddle quern.
This is called the Altar, and in this " cella " the
round stones are locally believed to be votive
offerings. These votive offerings of stones above

a well are not uncommon in the Highlands. This was evidently a praying station combined with a holy well. A similar well can be seen at Tobar Ashig, near Broadford in Skye. Such is the Rock of the Holy Women—remote, eloquent of the past, still revered, a place to dream in.

On the morning I left Canna we found our way down to the shore in the summer dark lit by the silver light of a full moon. Having boarded the motor-boat, we were soon racing out to the open sea. There we lay watching for the lights of the steamer as she rounded the point. The dawn was now coming up in all its mystery behind Skye. Over the Coolins there hung a white cloud, like incense rising to greet the sun. Soon every wave was washed with dawn, and the moon paled before the coming day. Then, the loom of the steamer towered above the heaving boat. A scramble on board. And the first beams of sunrise touched the cliffs of Canna with a rosy kiss.

VI

MEMORIES OF MULL :
I—THE EASTERN SHORES

I ONCE met a man on the road who entangled me in an argument. We could not agree. So at last I said :

" Why don't you use your imagination ? "

" Ay," he replied, " that's juist the difference between you and me—I dinna believe in tellin' lees."

And the man's reply gives us a very good idea of the popular meaning of imagination.

But I would rather go through the winter without a new coat than without some imagination. Men have been gifted with imagination that they might conjure up the truth of things. It is only when we pervert this divine gift that we begin to " tell lies " according to the argumentative tramp.

On dark December days the Scots climate is at its very worst. The atmosphere, which is a cross between a frost and a fresh, chills you to the bone. Streaks of sleety snow lie in the screes

of Caerketton. The east wind flies at your throat
like a wild beast whenever you turn the corner of
the street. On such days I often take out one
of my little oblong leather-backed note-books,
turn a few pages, shut my eyes, and lo ! I am
basking in the sunshine somewhere among the
Western Isles.

Mull is not very far from Oban. You can
see it from the window of every hotel. Yet
Mull is one of the islands that is still remote,
still unspoiled by trippers and charabancs ; and
the reason is not difficult to find. There are
only two piers where the steamer calls daily—one
at Salen, the other at Tobermory. The roads
are so bad that they make the average motorist
blaspheme. Moreover, the freight for motor cars
is very heavy, considering the short distance from
Oban. The tidal conditions also occasionally make
driving a motor car up and down the two planks
from the little steamer on to the pier so impossible
a task that, as one owner told me last summer, you
may find yourself and your car taken right up to
Ardnamurchan for the night before you can land
it at Tobermory with a more suitable tide the next
morning, and then drive back to your destination
at Salen. This only makes local hiring more
popular, unless you are staying a long time.

One more of these negative blessings.

Mull is such a wet place that the glens and moors are soppy, and the hills are green almost to the very top. Indeed, in a season of heavenly heat like last summer, we had to pay for every good day in August with an alternating bad one, and the rain in Mull can be as splendid as the sunshine. But, blessed be all these tribulations, for they have helped more than anything else to preserve the peace, the beauty, and the unspoiled glories of this wonderful island.

I never grow tired of the walk down the Sound from Salen. The whole history of the Western Isles seems to pass up and down the Sound of Mull as you saunter along this quiet road.

Just before coming to Forsa Bridge there is an intriguing path up the glen, past the cottage of Kilbeg, and over the bealach to Torness, in Glen More, with the mighty sides of Ben Taladh shadowing you on the right. Or if you take the way out of the glen to the right after leaving Kilbeg, you will find yourself at Loch Ba, and can then walk back to Salen. The sun was scorching when I made my way up to Kilbeg, and not a breath of air was stirring. I plugged on till I came to the spotless white cottage. If a place is called Kilbeg to-day, you can be sure that it marks the site of a

THE MOUNTAINS OF MULL

[To face page 52

little chapel which stood there hundreds of years ago. How many Highland welcomes I have had in a cottage up a Highland glen! The heat was burning on my cheek as I stood chapping at the door. I had a splendid thirst, and there was only one way to slocken it. So I asked politely if they had been churning recently, and soon I was sitting in the best of company drinking butter-milk, with tiny blobs of butter floating on the surface.

I then listened to the old, old story. All the stones of the chapel had been used long ago to build the walls of the large sheep fank and steading. I wandered over the site, went round the outer and inner walls of the fank and steading, in the hope of coming on some precious fragment. But there was nothing. All gone, like the people who lived in the glen. And now, nothing but dun deer, the nibbling sheep, and a few grouse on the green hillsides. Ben Taladh towered against the cloudless sky, like a silent sentry who watches over the dead generations of men, and will say nothing of what he has seen. The sound of the river was like a coronach. A sheep baa'd far up the green slopes. The eident woman was at her haymaking again. So, in the stifling heat I retraced my steps and made for Pennygown.

But at Forsa Bridge, instead of looking over

the parapet for trout, I stopped and spoke to two roadmen, who were cutting the overhanging trees with great sickle hooks lashed to eight-foot poles. I asked them if their weapons had been at Culloden.

Then we began to speak of a well-known Lord of Session, who was living at Forsa Lodge. Remembering a story which was once told of him in "The Juridical Review," I repeated it, to their great delight. When a young advocate he was at the Perth Circuit. An old poacher was up for trial, because game had been found on his person.

"Is there anyone to defend the prisoner?" asked the Judge.

Up got the young advocate.

"My Lord, I have here in my pocket two shillings and fourpence halfpenny. But, am I to be accused of having stolen the money just because it has been found in my pocket? And is my client to be accused of having stolen game just because rabbits have been found in his possession?"

And a verdict of not guilty was ultimately given.

Next year at the same Circuit the same hardened poacher was up for the same offence. The Judge asked again if there was anyone to defend the prisoner. There was silence in the Court. In vain the poacher looked round for his friend. Then he exclaimed :

" Whaur's the clever wee deevil wi' the muckle big heid that got me aff last year ? "

This time he went to prison.

One of the roadmen then retailed the story of a similar case in Argyll. A woman was accused of stealing a length of tweed from a local mill. The lawyer for the defence asked her before the trial to make a shirt for him of the same material, and a queer shirt it was. In Court he drew the attention of the Judge to the fact that he was wearing a shirt which had been made of the same tweed.

" Have I therefore stolen the tweed because this shirt is on my back ? "

And the woman got off.

Pennygown is my favourite resting-place on the Sound of Mull. You look right over to Fiunary, and down to Loch Aline and Ardtornish Castle, which, thanks to Sir Walter, reminds every tourist of the Lord of the Isles. Up the sound past Aros Castle to Ben Hiant and the dim blue hills of Ardnamurchan, from the shores of which Mingarry Castle looks down this haunted strait. And if you continue down the road past Craignure you will come to lordly Duart on its green point looking right across the Firth of Lorne to ivy-covered Dunolly. What a chain of historical castles—Dunolly, Duart, Ardtornish, Aros, Mingarry! How the beacon lights must have flashed the news from the one castle to the other when a hostile galley appeared in the west long ago!

There were priests in Pennygown then. Those were the men who raised the beautiful stone shaft which now stands within the ruined chapel, a dragon and galley on one side, and the Virgin and the Child on the other, with a riot of foliated ornament on both.

I went into the chapel and found a perfect poem of beauty in the corner of the little aumbry on the eastern wall. A bird had built its nest and hatched out her young close to where the altar must have stood. Immediately I seemed to hear monkish voices singing the psalm: "Yea, the sparrow hath found an house, and the swallow a nest for herself where she may lay her young, even thine altars, O Lord of Hosts, my King and my God."

Then I went down to the rocks, and, slipping into the cool green water, swam among the swaying weeds. Up again refreshed to light a fire on the shingle. The bread and cheese tasted better than a Lord Provost's banquet. The pungent smoke rose in the still air. There was a delicious fragrance of coffee. And after that, Sir Walter

Raleigh's delight, as I lay on the hot turf and dreamed of Fiunary.

All my life Fiunary has drawn my heart in the passing. You cannot see the manse so well as when I first sailed north, for the trees have grown up. But you can see the little church on the hill-side near Loch Aline. The present manse is not the original one mentioned in " Reminiscences of a Highland Parish."

Surely there never was a family in Scotland that gave so much to the Kirk in feet and inches and godly human nature as the Macleods of Morven! I sat in a college class with one of them who was between six and seven feet. One morning he told me that there had been a robbery at the manse of Govan, and the thief had stolen a number of boots.

" Silly thief," said I, " for no other family in Glasgow wears seven-leagued shoes."

The first Norman was ordained in Morven in 1775. He was the son of Macleod of Swordale, in Skye. There is no finer picture in the annals of the Kirk than the farewell which this first Norman took of his people when he was an old man. He had served his flock for over fifty years. It was Communion day in Morven, and the kirk was crowded. The tall, white-haired minister was

E

blind. Yet he had taught two generations to see the deep things of God. When he came from Skye long ago he had brought with him a whole host of retainers, according to the ancient custom. They all settled on the glebe or round the manse of Fiunary. One of them, Rory, had served the minister from the first day as faithful beadle and ghillie. Rory had only one eye, but it glittered like a gled's, and he could see more with it than any other man who had two. Now, like his master, Rory was old and bent.

The little fellow who sat in the manse pew that day and saw it all was the old minister's grandson. Many years after that, when he was the famous minister of the Barony, he wrote of this day. When Rory had shown the minister into the pulpit, he noticed that the blind old giant was facing the wrong way. So he went up the pulpit steps again, and reverently turned the mighty man of Morven round, guiding his hands on to the bookboard. There was a sound of weeping that day in the kirk when this blind old father in God spoke the solemn words of farewell to his beloved people.

Sixteen children were born to the first Norman in the manse at Fiunary. His son Norman became the minister of Campbeltown, from which he was translated to Campsie, and latterly to St. Columba's, Glasgow. He was the greatest Gaelic scholar of the day, and wrote many songs and poems, among them that song of deep pathos, "Farewell to Fiunary." He was Dean of the Thistle and Chapel Royal, Moderator of the Kirk, and the beloved friend of all Highlanders.

The third Norman in direct ecclesiastical descent became Norman Macleod of the Barony, the greatest of all the Macleods.

But it would take a volume to tell of all the other Macleods who have given their lives to the Kirk since 1775, and it would be a heartsome thing if someone would publish a complete and correct ecclesiastical record of this family. Five of them have been Moderators of the General Assembly. Three of them have been Deans of the Thistle. Dr. Norman of the Barony was also Chaplain-in-Ordinary to Queen Victoria, and one of her beloved friends. Dr. Donald, of the Park Church, Glasgow, if I mistake not, was Chaplain-in-Ordinary to three Sovereigns—Queen Victoria, King Edward VII, and King George V. Indeed, some years ago a writer to the newspapers calculated that the ordained ministries of the Macleods, when put together, amounted to 368 years. But the period must cover far more years than that now. Indeed, the first Macleod of Morven and his son, Dr. John Macleod, who was called the High Priest of Morven, served the parish between them for 107 years. Surely a record for the Church of Scotland. But one must never forget the tombstone of the two Torrances, father and son, in Glencorse Kirkyard.

When Dr. John Macleod of Morven and his nephew Norman went over to America in 1845 to visit the congregations of the Church of Scotland, they had many heart-moving interviews with exiled Highlanders.

" They laughed and cried turn about," wrote Norman of the Barony, " telling stories about the water-foot of Aros. . . . My uncle found a woman near Lake Simcoe who was longing to see him. When he entered she burst into tears. She had on a Highland plaid and a silver brooch. He thought he knew the brooch. It was Jenny Maclean's, the old henwife at Fiunary, given her by my uncle Donald before he died ; and this woman was Jenny's sister. It is like a resurrection to meet people in this way."

O Fiunary ! As I lie on the hot turf of Mull and gaze at your woods shimmering in the heat haze to-day, I think of the memories that must have welled up in the hearts of those Highland exiles long ago, when they thought of all that the manse of Fiunary meant to them! For, this hurt of home in the exiled Scot is a wound which nothing on earth can heal.

> " O hearts, to the hills of old memory true,
>   In the land of your love there are mourners for
>   you ;
>   As they wander by peopleless lochside and glen
>   Where the red deer are feeding o'er homesteads
>   of men."

VII

MEMORIES OF MULL:
II—THE WESTERN SHORES

THE west of Mull is the very outgait of heaven. To reach it, you have only to step across the few miles from Salen to Loch na Keal. But that is only the beginning. You can go by Tobermory and the Mishnish Lochs over the moors to Dervaig, and your descent to Dervaig will give you your heart's desire of hairpin bends, bad hills, and worse surfaces. Or you can travel up Glen Aros and down the little Bellart river to Dervaig.

My first recollection of Dervaig takes me back to the care-free days of youth. The anchor chain rattled out about two o'clock one summer morning at the mouth of Loch Cuan, somewhere about Quinish. We had been becalmed for two and a half days between Skye and Mull. I shall never forget the walk of a mile or two in the early hours of that beautiful June morning to Dervaig village. Then, a long wait at the local store until it was opened, and the long trail back with provisions for a quite ridiculous breakfast. Alas! The

THE WEST OF MULL AND INCHKENNETH

[To face page 62

itself on the west side is separated from the smaller island of Gometra by a mere strip of sea.

There are four things which everyone should remember about Ulva. The island was the seat of the MacQuarries. Dr. Johnson, after spending a night with the old chief of Ulva, records in his *Journal* that "in Ulva and I think nowhere else is continued the payment of *mercheta mulierum*, a fine in old times due to the laird at the marriage of a virgin. . . . MacQuarrie was used to demand a sheep, for which he now takes a crown." Ulva, also, was the original home of the family of David Livingstone; his grandfather was a crofter on the island; and his father left Ulva to settle at Blantyre. Here, long ago, was a College of Piping, where the MacArthurs taught the music of the great bagpipe. Lastly, Ulva is the scene of Thomas Campbell's poem, "Lord Ullin's Daughter":

> "O who be ye would cross Loch Gyle,
> This dark and stormy water?"
> "O I'm the chief of Ulva's Isle.
> And this Lord Ullin's daughter."

Campbell was a tutor at Sunipol, on the extreme north of Mull, and he would naturally know all this western seaboard.

The first of the MacArthurs was taught piping by one of the MacCrimmons of Skye. No pupil

Sir Walter Scott, married one of the Torloisk ladies, thereafter taking the name of Maclean Clephane. To-day, there are three Raeburns in Torloisk— one of Mrs. Maclean Clephane, one of the General, and one of their daughter Marion. Sir Walter used to visit this home of his soldier friend, and on one occasion he took with him another friend, Spencer John Alwyne Compton, the son and heir of the Marquis of Northampton. Scott has recorded that the daughters of Torloisk were the most learned and accomplished ladies he ever met. They were enthusiastic collectors of Gaelic songs and Highland music. They made original collections, writing down the songs or the melodies as they heard them. These were privately published for circulation among their friends. Sir Walter's friend, Alwyne Compton, married one of the learned ladies, and through this marriage the Torloisk estate came into the Northampton family. But she and her husband willed it so that it must always be heired by the younger son.

I wonder where these original collections of Gaelic songs and music are to-day !

Ulva is well called the Green Isle for it is a fine grassy sheep walk, with Ben Chreagach rising to a height of 1,066 feet. It is approached by a ferry that takes you across the narrow sound, and Ulva

The poor grassy road with its bad hills, sudden turnings, and beautiful views, leads you over the moors and down to the shores of Loch Tuath. If the day be fine you will see Staffa and distant Iona sleeping on the lap of the shining sea, with green Ulva and Gometra just across the loch. At Kilninian we sat on a heathery bank above the sea and basked in the sun, looking down on the Traigh na Kil, or the Church Strand. It was a lazy, unhasting lunch, and after it was over it seemed impossible to satisfy the soul with draughts of beauty.

Inevitably I wandered up to the church—a plain parish kirk which stands on the site of an older Celtic chapel. There, among the graves, I began the lifelong search for carved stones and found four of great interest; two foliated ones and two effigies; but all smothered in the long grass. I took off my coat, cut the grass, cleaned the stones, and took rough sketches.

Near Kilninian stands the historic house of Torloisk. Torloisk has been the home of a sept of the Macleans for centuries. The family was founded by Ailean na Sop, or " Alan of the Straws," who died in the sixteenth century—a long tragic tale which I cannot pause to relate. General Clephane, of Carslogie, in Fife, a great friend of auxiliary motor has now made all such adventure, impossible.

From Dervaig you set out for Calgary. Kilninian, Torloisk, and Ulva Ferry, and if you continue round the head of Loch na Keal by Gribun, Kilfinichen, and the head of Loch Scridain to Bunessan you are on your way to Iona. You will know by then what a means of grace bad roads can be, for you have to travel slowly all the way, and so the glory of the scenery sinks into the soul of those who love neither haste nor hurry. For seeing Mull or any other place on earth, nothing has ever been invented to take the place of a pair of legs. But alas ! legs are not always what they should be, and if you must travel by car to save time, pray often for the driver, for he will probably be cursing the ruts, and the shingle, and the wicked bends, and the impossible passing places, while you are dreaming carelessly of your heavenly surroundings.

Calgary Bay, with its white sands, its old grey castle among the trees, its green flats, and its wide vistas seawards to distant Coll and the Treshnish Isles, calls up memories of the exiled Highlanders who emigrated long ago from this beautiful corner of Mull, and named their new home in Canada after the earthly paradise which they had lost.

who was over the age of eleven was admitted to the College at Boreraig, and the course of instruction covered a period of fourteen years. When MacArthur returned to Mull he set up a College at Ulva.

As you continue round the head of Loch na Keal to Gribun, you will have plenty of time to gaze seawards, to Iorsa Isle and to the little holy island of Inch Kenneth, which Dr. Johnson very appropriately describes as " a proper prelude to Icolmkil," for it was called after an Irish saint who was a friend of St. Columba. Sir Alan Maclean and his two daughters entertained the great lexicographer in a little home of the utmost refinement, the chief asking Johnson to join in family worship, and " the elder of the ladies read the English service." The old chapel was entire in Johnson's day, and he describes the sanctuary, the graves, and a little Celtic bell which had remained there for ages guarded by the venerableness of the place. Then, he adds, " We could have been easily persuaded to a longer stay upon Inch Kenneth, but life will not be all passed in delight."

Thus, looking across to Inch Kenneth we remember that the while outward glories of life may pass away, the kindness of a human heart outlasts all else.

The road creeps below the angry cliffs of Gribun, which seem to threaten the traveller with annihilation should a fall of rock take place, for there is just room for the road between the cliffs and the sea which in stormy weather breaks in fury round this exposed coast.

Then the road cuts inland up Glen Seilisdeir to Kilfinichen on Loch Scridain. The rough triangle or promontory which the glen road cuts off is called Ardmeanach, one of the wildest spots in the Highlands. Not that the hills of Ardmeanach are very high, but that it is utterly desolate, remote from all roads, with a battlement of sea cliffs from Gribun to Burg which has defied the full force of the Atlantic from time immemorial. No wonder the ground on the cliffs here is called The Wilderness. To appreciate the cliffs you must view them from the sea, at dawning or sunset, when the great Atlantic swells are booming along the rocks, and making thunder in the caves. Little wonder that Ardmeanach is full of weird legends and uncanny tales of adventure. It was not by chance that the Victorian novelist William Black laid the scene of his tragic story, " Macleod of Dare," in this wild region; for the original of his " Castle Dare " is Burg Castle.

And yet, when you come down the glen road to

Kilfinichen Kirk, and find yourself between the delightful lands of Tiroran and the tree-clad parks of Killiemore, there is no hint of wildness. But as you travel round the head of Loch Scridain, past Pennygael, to a point on the road about three miles from Bunessan, you can look across the loch to the real magnificance of Ardmeanach, the wildest headland in Mull. You will then realise that Ben More and his mighty neighbours once formed one enormous volcano in action, on a far grander scale than the modern volcanoes of Italy. You can still count three distinct lava terraces on the flat top of Ardmeanach.

As you are about to cross the river at the head of Loch Scridain a road branches off to the left. This is the road that leads back through Glen More to Loch Spelve and the Sound of Mull. Glen More is a long and rather dreary glen, gloomy and green, and the road through it is rutty, grass-grown, and narrow, with little ditches which make it impossible for two cars to pass in many places. You will find Glenmore Lodge marked on the survey map, but to-day there is neither stick nor stone to mark the place where a lodge has stood, except it be at the solitary cottage of Ishriff. That, with Craig and Torness, are the only cottages in the whole length of the glen. At Torness a good

walker will find his way through the hills to Forsa,
near Pennygown on the Sound. There are no
trees in Glen More until you approach Ardura
and Loch Spelve. From Strathcoil to Kinloch,
or sea to sea, this road is (as the road book puts
it), " eleven miles of two tracks in gravel, and
grass between, but much used between Iona and
Grass Point." That remark was written many
years ago, and it is still up-to-date (1934).

This Glen More road was travelled by hundreds
of thousands of pilgrims who were making their
way to Iona from the south. They were ferried
across from Oban or some part of the mainland
to Grass Point on the south side of Loch Don ;
they walked all the way through Glen More, and
along the Ross of Mull to Fionnport ; then they
were ferried across the blue-green strait to holy
Icolmkil. There was no road of any kind then,
but that which was made by the tramp of many
feet. Even as late as 1843 there was no regular
road along the Ross of Mull, and the road through
Glen More had just been opened (1934).

One could linger over many other memories
of the island of Mull. For example, the leaf
beds of Ardtun, near Bunessan, where in 1850
the Duke of Argyll found most interesting beds
of fossil leaves. The once famous red granite

quarries opposite Iona from which great granite blocks were taken for buildings in London, Liverpool, Leeds, Edinburgh, and Glasgow—to London especially, where these blocks were used in the erection of the Albert Memorial, the Blackfriars Bridge, the Thames Embankment, Holborn Viaduct; and locally, for the building of Dhu Heartach and Skerryvore Lighthouses by the famous family of Stevenson. But for some of these business excursions, R.L.S. would never have laid the scene of *Kidnapped* in Mull.

After wandering in the west of Mull and then penetrating the long dreary length of Glen More, it is pleasant to find green lands and waving woods about Loch Buie, Loch Spelve, and Loch Don, a great demesne about Torosay Castle, and the ancient stronghold of Duart, which was rebuilt by Sir Fitzroy Maclean, the chief of the great Mull clan.

For over two hundred years the castle had remained empty, but in the year 1911 the 26th chief of the line found it possible to restore his bluff old keep of Duart. On the 24th of August, 1912, a great gathering of clansmen came from all parts of the world, to witness the recrowning of their chief and the rebirth of their clan. The outer walls are 14 feet thick, the inner 8 feet, and the

building itself is said to contain a hundred apart-
ments, great and small, above ground and below
ground. For centuries it withstood the stormy
blasts of war, as it has from time beyond memory
withstood the angry winds and waves. Now,
once more, it stands on its green promontory,
with the smoke rising from its chimneys, the silent
witnesses of an island story that is more than a
thousand years old.

VIII

A CEILIDH[1] IN SKYE: SONG AND STORY ROUND THE FIRE

It had been a wild, wet day. But, when the time of the Ceilidh arrived, the wind fell, the full moon rode out between the clouds, and the sheltered waters of the harbour became a silvered mirror. Far across the Sound, the lordly peak of Ben Screel rose dark above the waters of Loch Hourn. There was a lap of little waves along the shore, and the clean scent of sea wrack was wafted on the breath of winds that blew out of the mouth of night.

All along the roads little groups of men and women, from Teangue, Camuscross, and Duisdale, wended their way to the Ceilidh with laughter and the good Gaelic on their lips. Long level beams of light moved weirdly along the black hillsides, for many came in motor-cars from different parts of the island. Down at the harbour, by the little pier, there were greetings and handshakings, where a merry crowd waited until the door of the Ceilidh room was opened, and soon the benches were filled to overflowing.

[1] Pronounce *Kaylee*.

There was a pile of peats with a red glow in the centre of the floor. Everybody was there—lads and girls from the far-off crofts; the old school-master; the local piper; the policeman; hefty lads in their own tartans; some who were entire strangers; and others who had come back from the far-flung bounds of Empire. For, the piping, the ageless songs of the Celt, the sennachies with their tales—these still draw the Highland heart across the seven seas to the Ceilidh round the fire.

The Ceilidh has been the centre of Highland life for centuries. It was the story-telling round the fire and the social gathering of neighbours in winter time. At it stories and tales, ballads and poems were rehearsed and recited; songs were sung; conundrums were put; proverbs were quoted; and many other literary matters were dis-cussed. The old rule was that the houseman called on each person to tell a tale or sing a song. The kitchen of the old black house, with the peat fire in the centre of the floor, was the old-time scene of the Ceilidh. Old and young were there, and when the hour grew late, the children of the house, reluctant and resentful, were sent up the ladder to their shakedowns in the loft. But there was little or no sleep for them. When their elders were at their stories of the fairies, the glaisrig and the gruagach, or the dreadful water horse; their tales of Fingalian heroes who fought great battles and did mighty deeds—then many a little white-faced gillie lay in the loft, peering down through the trap-door with a shiver of fear at the weird tales of the fathers, and then laughed with glee when the piper struck up a rollicking port and the reel went round on the earthen floor.

Even in the eighteenth century few Highlanders, with the exception of the chiefs, had books or libraries. Sheer memory had to make up for the absence of the printed page. So, in every district there were sennachies, fine story-tellers, who could recite correctly from memory thousands of lines from the Ossianic poems, local history, legends of the Fayne, battle pieces of the Gael and the Norse invaders. There were also bards who could lilt and sing the stories of old romance, love, and tragedy. Many of these songs have come down to us, and are now preserved on printed pages with the music alongside.

We can well imagine, however, that the favourite tales would be those of the local clan fights in days when " a stream of blood separated the tartans " —Macleods of Dunvegan, Macdonalds of the

Isles, Macraes of Kintail, Mackenzies of Seaforth, Campbells of Lorne.

> " Great were the marvellous stories told
>   Of Ossian's heroes,
>   Giants, and witches, and young men bold,
>   Seeking adventures,
>   Winning king's daughters and guarded gold
>   Only with valour."

Now the old days lie far behind us. The Ceilidh, which is probably as old as the Celtic race, is a mere memory, unless in the Isles that lie nearest the sunset or in the glens which no high road will ever reach. That, however, makes us all the more thankful for what is left, and when at last the policeman stood inside the door of the crowded gathering-place the great night of music, song, and story began. Still and on, our thoughts went out across the unnumbered years, when we remembered the sennachies of old :

> " Our Winter's here, and mists through the glens
>   are trailing,
>   The constant rain-smirr rots the fallen leaf,
>   Lost in the years old Ossian's ghosts are wailing,
>   We'll bar the door and be alone with Grief ;
>   But, one last sprig of Highland heather's growing
>   Upon the Hills of Home that well you knew,
>   And it (oh, tell him, wind that's southward blowing),
>   My Wanderer, my Sennachie's for you ! "

The Celt of the Hebrides is born with music on his lips and tales in his soul. That night, there were eighteen different singers of songs and tellers of stories. Almost all of them were young, from crofts and cottages far and near. The Ceilidh is the most democratic of all gatherings, for all sorts and conditions meet round the peats as one family. There was no programme. There was no accompaniment of any kind to the songs. The houseman who sat by the peats simply called Donald Mhor or Ian Beg; John of the dogs or Mary of the cows; Little Catriona or the old Schoolmaster; the Doctor from the Soudan or the Lad from Kyle; the Hotel-keeper or the Piper. Each sang a song or told a story when called upon, with perfect willingness and a natural modesty. Of all the eighteen lads and girls who sang, each started off on the proper key, and kept to the lilt of the most intricate setting without loss of pitch or a single mistake.

There were laments like "Deirdre's Farewell," which is full of sadness; "Love Lilts," every note of which the company knew and crooned; rollicking "Dancing Songs," which were traditional substitutes for the pipes or the fiddle; histrionic songs like "Kishmul's Galley," sung with a Gaelic fire that set the blood tingling; comical "Catches," which made us all rock with laughter; ports on the pipes which well-nigh lifted the old rafters; and choruses which all sang with a rocking of the body. For the Celt sings with his body as well as with his soul, and I have watched the salmon fishers from one of the isles returning home on a Hebridean steamer, all joining hands and singing the songs of home, with a constant swaying of their bodies as an accompaniment to the croon.

The songs of the Ceilidh were all in the purest of Gaelic, with the soft lilt and grace notes which can never be quite acquired by Lowlanders, who have to *get up* the songs; for every one of them came from the lips and the heart of a lad or a girl who had drunk them in with their mother's milk. Such a feast of song, unaccompanied, spontaneous, and true to pitch, could not be provided by a similar company of country lads and girls in the Lowlands of Scotland. The Isles of the West are the Isles of Song. Music is the age-long heritage of the Hebridean Celt, and it is found all over the magic West, unless where it has been exchanged for a false gloom which has been imposed on the people through an utterly distorted idea of religion.

When the Ceilidh was over, it was a very happy company that wandered home along the hillsides by the shores of Sleat, under the white light of the moon. For, as the Gaelic old-word has it : " Night is a good herdman—he brings all creatures home."

The music kept singing in the heart. And as

we looked across to the hills of Glenelg, watched the
moonlight shimmering on the sea, and listened to
the sound of the distant pipes, the tears and laughter
of centuries seemed to well up within us. But
the song that stayed longest with us, and mingled
with our dreams, was " Deirdre's Farewell," the
oldest and saddest song of Gaeldom, so simple,
and yet, to those who know the tragedy that lies
behind it, and the music to which the words are
wed, as deep with longing as the pain of love has
ever reached :

> " Dearest Albyn, Land o'er yonder,
>   Thou dear land of wood and wave,
> Sore my heart that I must leave thee,
> But, 'tis Naoise I may not leave.
>
> O Glen Eite ! O Glen Eite !
>   Where they builded my bridal hold,
> Beauteous glen, in early morning
>   Flocks of sunbeams crowd thy fold.
>
> Glen da Rua ! Glen da Rua !
>   My love on all whose mother thou,
> From a cliff tree called a cuckoo,
>   And methinks I hear him now.
>   Glen da Rua ! Glen da Rua ! "

IX

ARDCHATTAN, KILMORE AND KILBRIDE : THREE GOD'S ACRES IN ARGYLL

An interest in ancient things need not end in mere dry-as-dust knowledge, but should bring us actually into touch with human life in remote ages. Even the scenery of any spot becomes reminiscent of those who once lived there, and I have yet to find anything that is more interesting than human nature. So the digger in the dust of history who cannot invest his stories with this living interest must always remain in a sense inhuman. These were thoughts which passed through the mind as the motor-boat chug-chugged up Loch Etive in the morning sunshine, for Deirdre's Lament seemed to be wafted down the centuries on the breeze from her own mountains and glens. To the end of time this will be Deirdre's Loch. To-day it is a dream of beauty, with Cruachan dominating its lower reaches and Starav lording it over its headwaters.

We were making for Ardchattan Priory. The September day was warm and quiet, and as we

stepped ashore we felt that we were in an ancient
haunt of peace. Immemorial trees; the ruins
of an old monastery; grey stones eloquent of
priors and priests long since dead; the slumbrous
sound of bees; smoke rising in a blue column
from the chimney of the Priory House, itself mel-
low with age. Add to these things one of the fairest
landscapes in Scotland, great mountains rising in
majesty across the waters of the loch; fields of
golden corn and little green meadows along the
wooded shores.

But the bones of history must come first. It
was away back in 1231 that Ardchattan Priory was
founded by Duncan MacKowle or MacDougal of
Lorne, and dedicated to St. Catan. As you saunter
below the great trees, and in the little precincts
of the monastery, you can almost hear the swish of
the monks' long garments in the lown of this September day. The choir is 66 feet long by 28 wide,
but it is very ruinous and part of the south-east
wall is gone. The double west wall is 9 feet
thick, and is pierced by an arch which leads into
a courtyard alongside the wall of the Priory House.
On the north side of the choir there is an oblong
irregular building which may have been the sacristy;
and to the south of the choir, enclosed by a wall,
is an open space, evidently a burial place. Within

are several monuments—two of them to priors of the MacDougal family, dated 1500 and 1502; but the inscriptions are now conjectural. An ambry in the east wall and a piscina under a recessed arch—that is all.

Many carved slabs, however, lie about: some broken, others defaced. One stone, split down the middle, has curious carvings, and may have been part of a cross. Another, standing upright, also split but clamped with iron, has two curious animals carved on it. Each faces the other; the one like a lion rampant with its tongue hanging out and a long pendant tail—the other like a unicorn with a stiff upright tail. A third is the effigy of a prior, but it also is cracked at the foot. I made a note of all three, but it is to be deplored that these precious stones in many parts of the Highlands are not better looked after.

Ardchattan Priory was well endowed under the diocese of Dunkeld, and many of the MacDougals of Lorne were priors. We read that there were " gardens and orchards " surrounded by " thorny-dykes and hedges," with tithes and " prior schotts " of the salmon fishings. King Robert the Bruce, after his fight at the west end of the Pass of Brander, held a Parliament at Ardchattan, when he took possession of the Land of Lorne. There were tulzies too at Ardchattan. In the 16th century the Priory passed into the hands of the Campbells, and in 1644 Colkitto Macdonald, that relentless raider, burned the priory when he laid waste the Campbell country. Old days and wild days, with the clash and clang of war.

The priory for a time seems to have escaped the ravages of the Reformation. But afterwards the crowds did great damage to many a beautiful building. The following letter speaks for itself. :

Traisr friendis, after maist hearty commendation, we pray you faill not to pas incontinentl to the Kyrk of . . ., and tak' doun the haill images therof, and bring furth to the Kyrk-zayrd, and burn them opinly. And sicklyke cast doun the alteris, and purge the Kyrk of all kynd of monumenta of idolatrye. And this see faill not to do, as ye will do us singulare empleaseyr, and so commitis you to the protection of God. Faill not but see tak' guid heid that neither dasks, windocks, not durris be ony way hurt or broken, eyther gassin-work or iron-work. Fie Edinburgh . . . 1560.

(Signed) Ar. Argyle.
James Stewart.
Ruthven.

So much for the bones of history. But the ancient is often grotesquely mixed up with the modern. As I stood among the long grass working on the stones I was opposite the windows of the kitchen premises which look directly on to the graves. Through one open window came a man's voice singing gaily a cockney ditty which he might have picked up in Leicester Square. Then, as one o'clock drew nigh, the scent of a delicious lunch was wafted out through the window, reminding me painfully of my own frugality. So I beat a retreat to the shore and ate my bread and cheese in the sunshine.

It is a quiet road that leads south from Connel Ferry to Loch Nell, or *Loch-nan-Eala*, the Loch of the Swans. You can take this road, or the road over the hills from Oban, and then turn northward from the head of Loch Feochan to Loch Nell. Either way it is about five miles. Almost at the south-west end of Loch Nell you will find the Serpent Mound close by the road.

It is a long mound with a double curve beautifully formed, the head lying to the west and the tail to the east. At first sight the casual observer might dismiss it with the remark that this is just an ordinary *eskar*, or a twisting ridge formed by post glacial gravel. But as you stand on the head and look along the curving mound there seems more in it than that.

So long ago as 1873, a world-wide authority— Dr. Phené—gave it as his opinion that here was a rude temple where the primitive inhabitants of Scotland practised *ophiolatry*, or Serpent Worship. The head is more expanded than the twisted body,

and when Dr. Phené opened the head he found a
cist or pre-historical burial, under a heavy boulder.
The cist contained 18 inches of charcoal, with a
knife-like implement made of chalcedony. All round
this ancient grave in the head was an immense
quantity of stones, many of which can be seen
to-day. Outside the mound there lay some boulders,
evidently the remains of a stone circle, with an
approach from the east that was marked by large
boulders on either side. Alas, most of these stones
have disappeared, having been broken up for building purposes. Along the ridge of the Serpent
Mound there were also smaller boulders, but they
too have disappeared. There is, however, an indica-
tion of a small cairn at the tail end of the mound,
and quite a number of other cairns used to be visible
in the near neighbourhood. I measured the mound
along its twisting ridge and found it 315 feet long,
from head to tail. When Dr. Phené read his paper
before the British Association in 1888 he declared
that the Serpent Mound at Loch Nell was the most
perfect serpent mound in the world.

What, then, does it all mean? It is certain that
the earliest inhabitants of this country worshipped
natural objects like the sun, trees, and wells. They
revered their dead and had some sort of shadowy
belief in another life. They even smeared their

dead with red ochre as a symbol of life and redemp-
tion. They worshipped the serpent also as a source
of wisdom and magic. Indeed, on the later Celtic
stones we find many and varied carvings of symbolic
serpents alongside of the Cross and Christian
symbols. Has not Dr. Alexander Carmichael translated an old Gaelic charm called Bride's Serpent ? :

> To-day is the day of Bride;
>   The serpent shall come out of his hole;
> I will not molest the serpent,
>   And the serpent will not molest me.

If you go on down the road from Loch Nell
and return to Oban without any further exploring,
you will miss two of the most interesting ruined
churches in Lorne—Kilmore and Kilbride. To get
to Kilmore you turn off the road a little way before
coming to Cleigh Inn; and you continue on the
Oban road for a couple of miles and take the Lerags
road to the left to get to Kilbride. Oban was in
the united parishes of Kilmore and Kilbride when
that metropolis of the west was a mere clachan;
and its people had to walk to Kilmore or Kilbride
if they wished to attend their parish churches.

I will not linger over the old stones of Kilmore,
but will rather recall a quaint description of a
Sunday at Kilmore by Mrs. Grant of Laggan in her
" Letters from the Mountains " :

We set out on horseback in a shower of snow, which people here mind no more than hair powder. . . . This was an odd old church, almost ruinous. But when the preacher came in he roused all my attention. I never beheld a countenance so keenly expressive, nor such dark piercing eyes. He is very like his sister F. M.[1], and resembles her in a superior musical genius. . . . When I began to look about, the dresses and countenances of the people presented new matter for speculation. . . . I could not spare a look to the young people, so much was I engrossed in contemplating their grandmothers. They preserve the form of dress worn some hundreds of years ago. Stately, erect, and self-satisfied, without a trace of the languor or coldness of age, they march up the area with gaudy-coloured plaids fastened about their breasts with a silver brooch like the full moon in size and shape. They have a peculiar lively blue eye, and a fair fresh complexion. Round their heads is tied the very plain kerchief Mrs. Page alludes to when Falstaff tells her how well she would become a *Venetian tire*: and on each cheek depends a silver lock which is always cherished and considered, not improperly, as a kind of decoration. These people you must observe were the common people; the old *ladies* were habited in the costume of the year one. . . . Why should I introduce you to the cynoshure of the assembly, the old major with his tartan coat, his large silver buttons, worn in Montrose's wars by his grandfather, and his redundant silver locks adorning a countenance the picture of health and benignity. Nor will you care a farthing for his three thin upright sisters, though they are, amidst their oddity, very like mountain gentlewomen: nor for his nine cousins. . . . If I were to stay and frequent this church for a twelvemonth . . . I doubt not that I might be qualified to compile a heraldry of Lorn, so skilled should I become in its antiquities.

Alas, what ghosts of those fine old Highland gentle-folk haunt the wind-blown graves of Kilmore to-day!

[1] Rev. Peter Macdonald—Brother of Flora Macdonald.

As you step down the by-road to Kilbride, you seem to have wandered into one of those little valleys reminiscent of a world long since gone. Green hills, a winding road, a ruined church, a great God's acre round it, in which lie the remains of many of the old Lorne families, a glimpse of Loch Feochan at the foot of the valley, and beyond that a barrier of low hills. Dominating kirk and homestead stands a great Celtic Cross on a knoll above the road.

I first came on this paradise of peace many years ago when I was walking from Ardrishaig to Oban. I continued my journey to that town by an ideal route—along a hill path—across the waters of Lochan na Bhreathrach by a little bridge; on to Gallanach; across the ferry to Kerrera and Castle Gylen: and back across the sound by ferry and so by road to Oban. At that time the Cross was lying in three bits, utterly neglected. Now it is beautifully restored. In the churchyard I counted nine stones with the remains of fine tracery on them. But the Cross once more dominates Kilbride, for it has been re-erected on its ancient site—a little hill as you approach Kilbride through the *bealach*. The spot is known as *Bealach-an-t'-sleuch-daibh*, or the Place of Prostration. In olden times the Cross was called the Kneeling Cross. It stands 11 feet high, and the three pieces have now been carefully assembled, cemented, and enclosed in a fine metal frame. At the top of the south side, there is a crucifix with I.H.S. above it, and lower down there is an inscription in Gothic which reads : *Archibaldus Campbellus Laerig mi fieri anno D.M.* 1516. Underneath is a horse-like animal with Celtic tracery springing from head and tail. At the foot are the initials S. McD. in more modern lettering. The other side of the Cross is one mass of intricate tracery.

So we end our wanderings at the Cross which casts its kindly shadow over kirk and homestead, beside the *bealach* which leads us to the place of peace.

G

X

CORRIEVRECHAN : THE BOILING CAULDRON

In the old days, before sailing boats were fitted with auxiliary motors, it was with a somewhat fearful eye you stood on the deck, when the wind was dying, and gazed across the swirling tides to Corrievrechan, the little strait that lies between Scarba and Jura. It was quite enough that you had to pass through the tides of the Dorus Mor, the Great Gate of the sea which lies off Craignish Point. In those days you had to calculate the tides to a nicety, else you might be tossed about in the countless eddies like a cork. Now, even in a small boat, if there is a good motor engine, you can afford to go easy about the tides, and the Dorus Mor has very largely lost its terrors. But Corrievrechan is another story. However, where there is a spice of danger there is always an added zest to the adventure. So one afternoon in April we set out from the House of Hospitality in a motor boat to visit " The Hag," or *Cailleach*, as the Celts called this cauldron of the speckled seas.

THE PAPS OF JURA

[To face page 90]

Corrievrechan is seven or eight miles north-west
of Crinan. We left to get there in plenty of time,
so that we might get in and out of the gulf in slack
water. The strait is only half a mile across, from
the south tip of Scarba to the north tip of Jura.
From the point of Craignish there runs southwards
a little line of lonely islands—Garbh Reisa, the
Eilean na Cill group, and Eilean na h'Eairne. Our
way lay right through them, and past another
island—Reisa an t'Sruith—which lies nearer Corrievrechan. Almost all this sea is a whirl of tides
when the race is on, but only in Dorus Mor and in
Corrievrechan is there any real boiling of the waters.
When, however, to the strong run of the tide is
added a stiff opposing wind, the jabble is at its very
worst.

And yet, the panorama of mountains, islands,
and seas from Crinan is hard to beat on the west
coast of Scotland. Behind Jura and Scarba, and all
the Isles of Lorne, there rise the far off mountains
of Mull. In clear weather the sun sets most glori-
ously. The whole sky is awash with delicate colours,
from the dusky blue of the empyrean down through
every shade of green, amethyst, and pink, to the
heavenly crimsons where the red ball of fire dips
behind the gulf : and the sea reflects the magic
colours of the sky. All the nobbly little hills of

Lorne are picked out in the lights and shadow of the after-glow; the islands floating in the opalescent sea take on a soft plum colour; and the mountains of Mull become mere whiffs of blue.

Before the advent of the motor car almost all the tourists in Scotland sailed down the Clyde and up Loch Fyne to Ardrishaig, through the Crinan Canal on the " Linnet," and then set out on a sail for Oban through the Isles of Lorne—a day of unparalleled beauty. Now the tourist is whisked away on a charabanc from Ardrishaig to Oban, and I suppose few people have any idea of the glory of the lochs and islands of Lorne.

On the still summer days I have lain on the point of Craignish, or on the hills above Ardifur, listening to the constant roar of Corrievrechan five or six miles away, and I have watched through a pair of strong glasses the tidal seas leaping up in great white columns of spray. When the vortex is at its worst and the whirlpool is lashed into fury by leaping seas and contending winds, then the place is impossible for a small boat.

Even when sailing in on the slack of the tide on this April day, there was a certain amount of suppressed excitement; for the waters still swirled in oily serpent-like circles, which had an evil fascination about them. But having sailed in, there was an equal sense of relief when we sailed out again. It was like stealing into a lion's cage and tickling the sleeping lion, which at any moment might waken up and devour you.

Needless to say, there are many legends about Corrievrechan. Adamnan, in his "Life of St. Columba," calls it *Charybdis Brecani*, or Brechan's Cauldron. The Columban story is that Brecan, the son of Maine, the son of Niall of the Nine Hostages, was engulfed in it. The *Charybdis* referred to, however, may have been the tidal race between the coast of Erin and the Isle of Rathlin. In any case, it is said that Columba, passing through the cauldron, saw the bones of Brecan cast up by the whirlpool, at which he exclaimed, "This is friendly of thee, O aged Brecan!"

The Norse version of the story is that Brecan was the son of the king of Lochlin (Norway), and to prove his devotion to his lady love he promised to spend three days and three nights at anchor in the cauldron. The wise men of Lochlin advised him to cast out three anchors and to secure them to his galley with three ropes, one of wool, another of hemp, and a third made of the hair of women of spotless fame. The first night, the woollen rope broke; the second night the hempen rope broke; and the third night, just when the vigil was about to end, one of the hairs parted, and gradually the remaining hairs gave way. So the Prince and his galley and all who were in it went down to the bottom of the cauldron. But the Prince had a faithful dog, which kept watch over him, and when the sea gave up its dead the black dog dragged Brecan ashore, and the Prince was buried in Uamh Bhreacaini, or the Cave of Brecan, on the shores of Jura.

This wild region must have been the scene of many a tragedy on land and sea. Indeed, in a cave on the shore of Glengarrisdale Bay, not far from Corrievrechan, there was found within living memory the skull of a warrior. The bonnie fighter must have died with his face to the foe, for two deep gashes were found on the frontal bone. One had cut a disc of bone right off, the other had pierced the skull above the temple.

But the real interest in Corrievrechan lies in the question I have often asked—" What makes this narrow channel between Scarba and Jura such a raging cauldron of water?" The answer is clear enough. The tremendous tides from the Irish Channel run up daily into the narrow basin formed by Islay, Jura, Scarba, and Luing on the one side, and on the other by Kintyre, Knapdale, and Craignish. This basin is so confined that the mass of water which forces its way through the narrows of Corrievrechen rushes at a speed of eleven knots an hour. Add to this two facts—first, that on the floor of the gulf there is a cliff-like break in the rocks, over which the water falls to a great depth, for the soundings vary suddenly from 50 to 90 and then to 150 fathoms ; and, second, in the middle of this rocky floor there is a huge stack or pyramid of rock, the top of which is actually within 15 fathoms of the surface water. So when this stream of ocean is running at its greatest velocity, a spout of green water shoots into the air from the hidden deep and causes whirlpools in the surging seas. Local sailors have told me that in the upright stack of rock there is a great hole, through which the sea bores down and up again and again. But this tale seems far fetched. Add to all these turbulent elements a strong wind opposing the strong tide, and the jabble of Corrievrechan is complete. The roar of the waters can be awe-inspiring.

We sailed back to the little group of Eilean na Cill Islands, and the boatman steered us into a land-locked haven among the rocks, where you can ride at anchor in safety. The seals were nosing about in the tidal waters which are full of fish. Once on these islands the boatman heard a strange sound on a still day, as if someone was singing in the solitude. So he crept over the rocks, and, looking down, saw a mother seal crooning to her young. The seals are the children of the king of Lochlin, but when they sing it is the Gaelic that they like best.

On the highest part of the island we had tea, and sat gazing at the seals and at the tidal currents which had already set in. The very islands about us spoke of these streams of the sea; for Eilean Reisa means the Race of the Tide; and Eilean an t' Sruith means the Isle of the Running Water. Here also on this lonely isle where we sit, a hermit lived in Columba's time, so it also is called the Isle of the Holy Church.

We set out on the return, and the *Beannachadh Cuain*, or ancient sea prayer of the Celts, was on our lips. The words may have been used by some of the early missionaries of Christ, who often crossed these tidal seas in their skin coracles at the risk of their lives:

> Carry us over the surface of the sea,
> Carry us safely to a haven of peace,
> Bless our boatman and our boat,
> Bless our anchors and our oars,
> Each stay and halyard and traveller,
> Our mainsails to our tall masts
> Keep, O King of the elements, in their place
> That we may return home in peace;
> I myself will sit down at the helm,
> It is God's own Son who will give me guidance
> As He gave to Columba the mild,
> What time he set stay to sails.

XI

THE SILKEN GOWN: A BLUE DAY
AT SEA

THE secret of happiness is to aim high and yet to be content with what you ultimately get. Or, as the Scots proverb put it, " Bode for a silk gown and you may get the sleeve o't."

It was in that spirit I rowed out from Crinan all alone in a modest dinghy. As every lover of the west knows, the panorama of islands and seas about Crinan is one of indescribable beauty. The mountains of Mull on this quiet August day were a mere whiff of purple against the summer sky. Scarba and Jura watched the tides of Corrievrechan growling between them. Nearer still, the long low bluff of Craignish Point thrust itself into the sea where the Dorus Mor—that water gate to all a sailor's joys—a mere half-mile of water, raced between the point and the little island of Garbh Reisa.

" Bode for a silk gown," I kept repeating to myself as I rowed out in perfect happiness, and still further out, into the pearly seas. The breeze freshened, and was now rippling the water into a deeper blue. So, I shipped my oars ; stepped one of them through the mast hole in the forward thwart ; ran up my Burberry for a sail ; tied a stout piece of string to the tail of it ; sat down in the stern with an oar over the counter for a rudder ; and soon I was puffing the pipe of peace as I set a course for the infinite, at a speed of one knot per hour. I had often wished for the Silken Gown—spelled in capitals. Sitting here in the little dinghy I knew I had only got the sleeve of it—spelled in very small letters.

Yonder, away down the Sound of Jura, I could see the gleam of white wings as a lordly yacht came bowling up to the north with every sail set to catch the freshening breeze.

" And that," said I with a laugh, " is the Silken Gown."

Well, the days of silken gowns were long over for me. Often when I have sailed the dinghy with a Burberry, an oar, and a few bits of string, my consolation has been that the blessed winds of God can fill all kinds of sails, whether they be towering clouds of snowy canvas or a little brown rag ; and, when it comes to navigating the seas of this world, there may perhaps be as much happiness in the " Sleeve o't " as in the " Silken Gown " itself.

So I gradually crept out to Ardnoe Point. At long last I got there. What a blessed change this ploutering about all alone at sea is to a man who, when at home, lives night and day by a time-table, and keeps rushing about from one affair to another with a pathetic dab at some larger duty between times! The Silken Gown was now racing up the Sound, and it would never do for those on board her to see from their snowy decks an elderly dreamer working his way homeward like a madman with a Burberry and a bit of string. I know from experience how awkward a pair of binoculars can be at sea.

I landed on the shore of Ardnoe Point to visit the Sailor's Grave. It is a lonely spot, and the little headstone stands on a green howe looking across to Jura and Corrievrechan with its eternal roar. The inscription tells its own story. " Erected by Isabella Eston in memory of her husband John Black, feuer and fishcurer in Greenock, who died of cholera on board his schooner *Diana*, and was interred here, 28th July, 1832, aged 45 years."

There are similar sailors' graves round our lonely coasts; for in the old days when cholera claimed a victim on board ship, the dead sailor was buried on the nearest point of land, provided it was far enough from a dwelling place or the local churchyard. Highland people have always had a superstitious dread of infectious disease.

By the time I had finished a frugal tea the Silken Gown was coming round the point. I immediately launched the dinghy, and rowed out to see her as she passed.

Those who have never gone down to the sea in ships in the days when sails were sails, and sailors knew how to handle them, will never know the thrill of watching a stately ship go by; with every one of her snowy sails drawing to perfection; the seas curling in green curves from her cut-water; a wash of foam on her lee quarter; and the wind singing eternal sea chanties in her shrouds. Read John Masefield's "Bird of Dawning," and if you are a sailor with any sentiment in you, when you come to the description of the race between the two China clippers thrashing up the English Channel, the tears will be in your eyes with the sheer emotion of that epic of the lost days, when *Thermopylæ* and *Cutty Sark* crowded on every stitch of canvas to win the blue ribbon of the seas.

So the dreamer sat in the little Sleeve and watched the Silken Gown go by.

But the House of Hospitality is a wonderful gathering ground for sib souls. So, after a day or

two of friendship and sea gossip, we all went
aboard the Silken Gown. She lay at anchor behind
the island in the Bay of the Port, with her white
hull, white decks, a great spread of snowy canvas,
and shining spars. As I looked up at the peak of
her Bermuda mainsail, I thought of the old days
when Malcolm used to be sent up the ratlines to
lace or unlace the topsail. But rigs, like other
things, have changed, and I wondered what would
happen if in a sudden squall they had to shorten
sail. The Silken Gown was ketch rigged, and it
was like coming home after half a lifetime's exile
to look round the decks and cast a glance aloft.

What a happy party sat in the cockpit watching
the blue world of islands and seas slip by on that
radiant summer day! All the sounds were so
familiar. The wind in the rigging; the creaking of
blocks; the sweesh of the seas racing past her lee
quarter; the slap of an occasional sea on her
bows, with the sting of salt spray on the cheek;
and the old happy scream of the seabirds! We
sailed up the eastern shores of Loch Craignish,
which is surely the most beautiful sea loch in
Nether Lorne. Yonder at the head of it stands
Barbreck House, a bluff square mansion with
many eyes which flash and twinkle in the sunset,
and look down the whole length of this loch with

its magnificent vista of islands and craggy hills. We then fetched across to Ardfern Bay, took a circle round the tiny island, and set out again on the long reach home.

It was all very well lying about in laziness watching the sea, the sails, the clouds, and the other men working the Silken Gown. I sat wondering and waiting in silence and with a fearful expectancy. Would the moment ever come? Just then it arrived.

" Take a turn at the tiller now."

Outwardly I was quite calm. But, inwardly, it was a thumping joy as I thought of the Burberry and the " Sleeve o't." After all these years I took the long slender tiller in my hand, and lo! she answered to the touch like a sensitive lover. The years fled away, and I was back again on the west of Skye, beating against the wind and wave, bareheaded in the rain, trying to keep the old schooner on her proper course.

Then the breeze suddenly freshened. As we bowled along between the islands she lay over until her lee rail was well under the water. I glanced up at the Bermuda sail, and thought of the little topsails of old. But the fever was racing through my blood as the Silken Gown was racing through the water, and I did not like to yield a

LOCH CRAIGNISH AND CASTLE

[To face page 102

single point. A great sea broke over her, and the spray swept us from end to end. I had forgotten all about the ladies.

" Let her up a bit," cried the owner with a laugh.

So, reluctantly, putting down the helm I luffed her into the wind a point or two to ease her.

The wind held until we were into the mouth of Loch Crinan, and the Silken Gown raced all the way home. The splendid trick was over. As we approached the sheltered waters behind the island the wind took off, the anchor went out, and soon the white wings were folded. Down came the great Bermuda sail. It was soon rolled. The gaskets were tied. The cover was put on. Every rope was coiled. A sailor is the tidiest man in the world.

Then, down below to the cosy saloon to splice the main brace and have a hearty tea. And that night, after the sun had gone down in all its glory, the stars came out, and we walked to the brow of the road behind the House of Hospitality, and looked down on the anchorage. There, in the purple night lay the Silken Gown at rest, with her riding light making a long golden reflection in the still water.

> " The hushed sea seems to hold her breath,
>   And o'er the giddy swaying spars,
>   Silent and excellent as Death,
>   The dim blue skies are bright with stars."

He who wrote these words knows the secrets of the sea. So, that night I fell asleep with one of his sea songs on my lips, thankful that for one day again the clock of time had been put back, and the old love of the sea had made me young again.

"I must go down to the seas again, to the lonely sea and the
    sky,
And all I ask is a tall ship and a star to steer her by,
And the wheel's kick and the wind's song and the white
    sail's shaking,
And a grey mist on the sea's face and a grey dawn breaking.

I must go down to the seas again, for the call of the running
    tide
Is a wild call and a clear call that may not be denied;
And all I ask is a windy day with the white clouds flying,
And the flung spray and the blown spume, and the sea-
    gulls crying."

XII

LOCH KILLISPORT : NOVEMBER MEMORIES

To-day, November is at its very worst. A gale of wind is roaring across the city. The streets are swept by sheets of cold rain, and to add to the dolour of the day, black clouds have rolled up until noontide is like midnight. Thunder claps are now pounding the earth like heavy guns, and the rain has redoubled its fury.

As I look out of my window, I can see a great birch tree in the garden opposite. When November comes that tree is one of my winter blessings, for when I gaze at its golden glories I am transported to the glens, and moors, and woodlands where, on a wild wet day like this, the whole world is red and gold. Now the birch is waving thousands of golden shekels with a shiver of beauty against the storm. Beauty is as necessary to a healthy soul as food is to a healthy body. Once, when this tree stood with its pure gold gleaming in the sunshine of a still November day, I ran away. Before night, I was in the middle of one of the

wildest deer forests in Scotland, listening to the
sound of rushing waters under the stars ; and
next morning I wandered in the sunshine over hills
and moors, and through birch woods, revelling
in the colour of the dying world which was splashed
with every shade of brown and red and gold.

So, to-day, when the storm lashes the earth
with its wild wet whips, I turn away from the
streaming windows, sit down at the fire, put on a
very old pair of magic spectacles, and bring some
beauty back from May to November.

What miracles are wrought every year in the
month of May! After weeks of cold winds and
tempestuous weather, we set off on the old trail
in perfect sunshine. At Dalmally we had forgotten
all our cares. At Inveraray we were in a world of
green woodlands, blue seas, and old-time memories.
All down Loch Fyne the swirling white clouds
were reflected in the mirror of calm water. As we
turned the corner at Loch Gilp our faces were set
westwards, and at Crinan that night the sun went
down behind Jura, Scarba, and Mull with a heavenly
glory which was beyond all words beautiful.

Next morning the rock garden was blazing with
colour. The birches and larches of Knapdale
made a delicate green mist, like a bridal veil,
along the hillsides. Yet the veil was so diaphanous

that it did not hide a single grey stem or the russet
leaves which autumn had laid below the trees.
It was a delight to walk the good earth on a carpet
of primroses, violets, and bluebell buds. Indeed,
it was hard to pick your steps for beauty. All the
old pleasures which have made the men of every
generation sing for joy in spring were here—
bird music on the hills, green woods, dancing seas,
the dazzle of snowy clouds against the blue, the
infinite panoramas of the Isles of Lorne and the
Bens of Jura, great pillars of smoke rising from
the moorburn which was late this year owing to
the wet spring, lambs gambolling in sheer delight
on the grass, and the happy sound of streams
whose waters were crystal clear. These are some
of the May miracles which have always thrilled
the heart of man.

I have visions of radiant hours spent on the
west coast of Kintyre, looking out upon the
shimmering seas from green machairs or silver
sands; of palm trees growing at Ronachan and
Killean; of the great flats of Rhunahaorine, near
Largie Castle, where Colkitto fought a battle;
of exploring an ancient *dun* above the shore at
Corriechrevie.

But nothing could be more heartsome to remember in the dreary winter-time than one day when

we took the Kilberry road along West Loch
Tarbert by Achaclachgach and Ardpatrick. We
were making for Loch Killisport and Columba's
Cave at Cove, near Ellary, and we stopped for a
while at little Loch Stornaway to examine two
standing stones. It is a short loch, with white
sands at its head and a beautiful outlook to the
sea, past the north end of Gigha. This lonely bay
seems to speak of

> "Old, unhappy, far off things,
> And battles long ago."

for here were the silent yet eloquent standing stones,
and here was a great Norseman's *vik* or harbour—
" Stjarna's vik "—when he was sailing among the
western isles with his galleys.

The road then takes you north along the sea
front, past Kilberry Castle, Ormsary House, and
Baranlongart, right round the head of the loch
to Achahoish. Instead of continuing on the main
road over the hills to Inverneil, on Loch Fyne,
you carry on to the left until the road becomes the
private avenue to Ellary House.

The avenue winds along the shore between little
tree-clad rocks on the one side, and on the other
side the sea. Not far from the lodge gate stands
the ruined church of Columba on the green sward.
Only part of the gables and a wall remain, but in

the beauty of that May evening we realised what a genius the early Celtic missionaries had for choosing their haunts of peace. Needless to say, the church must have been built hundreds of years after Columba's time ; for, like many of the ruined chapels in the district, it has Norman features ; so that would date it from about the middle of the twelfth century.

Having obtained permission to explore Columba's Cave, we received the key at the lodge, walked a little beyond the ruined church, and found the cave in the face of the cliff, all draped with the fresh greenery of spring. Very properly the entrance is protected by a rough fence with a locked gate in it. The cave itself is formed by one vast rock leaning against another, or at least appearing to do so. It is clean and dry and very well kept. On entering, you see a high flat ledge to the right, and you climb up to this rock platform by means of a wooden ladder. On this ledge a rough stone altar is built, and above the altar on the wall of the cave a little Latin cross is carved. On the flat rock floor to the right of the altar a stoup for holy water has been hollowed out. Several little holes have been bored on the wall of the cave as if another later cross or some holy relic had been fixed there.

The local tradition is that Columba, on leaving Ireland, landed here and made his abode in the cave; but one day, on ascending a neighbouring hill, he caught a glimpse of Ireland, from which he had been banished. So he straightway sailed further north and landed on Iona. From its only hill it is impossible to see Ireland. Therefore, Columba stayed on Hi.

The two great founders of the early Christian Church in Scotland were St. Ninian and St. Columba. St. Ninian's Cave, near Glasserton, in Galloway, has several primitive crosses carved on its rock wall; and here in St. Columba's Cave at Loch Killisport we find one primitive cross on the wall. These two caves are surely unique, for it is quite possible that each contains a cross that was carved by the Saint's own hand.

So we passed up the 'longshore avenue in the quiet of the early evening. Ellary is surely one of the fairest policies in the West Highlands, with its wealth of trees, its almost tropical plants, and its beautiful dwelling set in velvet lawns above the sea. I was anxious to see the little burial-ground at Cladh a Bhile beyond the mansion house. Having obtained minute directions, I set out along a woodland path, which came to a loose end at an iron gate. I carried on too far, so I had to retrace

my steps. There are, however, no ancient carved
Celtic slabs here, such as you will find in abundance
over the hill at Kilmory Knap, on Loch Sween.
It was now growing late, and we had a long way to
go. But my thoughts of Ellary will always be happy
and fragrant, because of its prodigal wealth of
flowering azaleas. The air was drugged with their
sweet scent. The sun was near its setting. As we
passed down the long seaside avenue, the golden
tangle, the whispering trees, the shimmering sands,
the old chapel, and the holy cave with the Columban
cross—all these mingled our memory of ancient
things with the fragrance of living flowers, and
filled us with a strange sense of reminiscence.

XIII

THE CHIN OF MACMARQUIS : THE ISLAND OF SEIL

" The wisdom of a learned man cometh by opportunity of leisure : and he that hath little business shall become wise."

THESE words came to mind as I sat through the drowsy afternoon in a garden of delight. Although a strong wind was ruffling the waters of the loch into a plain of sapphire, not a breath invaded this pocket of peace. The steep rock garden behind me was still full of colour. In front of me stood two great bushes of lavender with bees working on the purple blooms, and a white butterfly flitting from flower to flower. No garden is complete without the hum of bees. For a tired man this is paradise—to have the opportunity of leisure : to sit in the sunshine ; just to look at things, and listen to the drone of bees, while the beauty soaks in. For a hard worker, however, there is more than mere pleasure in the drone of bees : there is a warning, too : for the average bee works itself to death. So let the white butterfly instruct him that when work has to be done, it is better to do

CLACHAN BRIDGE, ISLE OF SEIL

[To face page 112]

it as airily as possible, without haste or hurry. Every man has his own way of taking rest, and my pilgrimage on the morrow is to be a trek through the Land of Lorne to see if the Chin of Macmarquis is still there !

.   .   .   .   .

It was a heavenly summer day, and all through its happy hours I beheld

> "Ridge and gulf and distant ocean
> Gleaming like a silver shield."

Had I lingered over every place of interest on the way, I would never have got there—Dunadd, with its ancient kings ; Kilmartin, beautiful for situation ; Craignish, the loveliest of all the Lochs of Lorne ; the fascinations of Asknish Bay ; Melfort, with its bosky woods ; and a host of other favourite haunts. But at Kilninver I turned to the left up the steep hill road that leads to the Island of Seil and Easdale. Instead of continuing along the road to Ardmaddy Castle, the road to Seil turns sharply to the right at Auchnasaul, and another half-mile brings you to one of the most interesting old bridges in Scotland.

Clachan Bridge is famous locally for being the only bridge in the world that spans the Atlantic. But the Atlantic here is a very narrow stream.

The Sound of Seil, between the island and the
mainland of Lorne, gradually narrows until it is
a long, thin, river-like bit of sea water, racing
northwards or southwards according to the flow
or ebb of the tide. At low tide you can see the
immense growth of tangle which makes the passage
of a boat very unpleasant, especially a motor boat
with a propeller. The bridge is a steep one, with
a span of 70 feet, and 40 feet above the bed of the
channel. It was completed in 1792 from plans by
Telford, the famous bridge builder. It stands to-day
as strong as ever; but the stones of the foundations,
bare at low tide, would be none the worse of a little
cement. Over the bridge, and you are on the Island
of Seil. Like all the Isles of Lorne, it is a green
island, four miles long and two across, its highest
hill just under 400 feet. West of Seil, across a
very narrow sound, lies the little island of Easdale,
centre of the slate industry. But this industry so
dominates the whole district that the road across
Clachan Bridge is for all the world the road to
Easdale.

Little over a mile from Easdale there is a clachan
called Kilbride. As the name indicates, there
was in olden times a church here dedicated to
St. Bride, and the lands round this sacred shrine
were all Church lands. The family of Maclachlan

was closely associated with the church at Kilbride
in those days, one Farquhar Maclachlan being the
last Bishop but one before the Reformation. A
great many of this family had been Vicars of
Kilbride. So when the Church lands were confis-
cated at the Reformation the lands of Kilbride
were given to Patrick Maclachlan, who became a
Protestant. The Maclachlans were not only an
ecclesiastical race, but a very scholarly family.
They loved the literature of the Highlands, and
made a collection of manuscripts which are very old.
These are now in the National Library at Edinburgh.

It is a far cry from medieval manuscripts to
the slate industry, and when you come to Easdale
you are in the region of one of the most prosperous
trades left in the Highlands. A little bay with the
clean white cottages of Eilean a Beich running out
to the point of Seil under the steep cliffs of Dun-
more; an ample pier; heaps of slate everywhere; and
a very narrow channel 150 yards broad separating
Seil from the small island of Easdale, where there
is another village on the point—to all that add
an incomparable view seawards to the isles of
Lorne and the mighty ramparts of Mull, and you
have Easdale.

As early as 1549 Dean Munro mentions the
neighbouring island of Belnahua as " ane iyllane

. . . quharin ther is fair skailzie (slates) aneuche."
But, while he mentions Easdale (calling it Eisd-
calfe), he makes no reference to its "skailzie"
or slates. There is a tradition, however, that
Castle Stalcaire, in Appin, was roofed with Easdale
slates when it was built in the reign of James IV
of Flodden memory (1513); and it is said that
Ardmaddy Castle, on the mainland opposite Seil,
was re-roofed with them in 1676. Indeed, some of
the pine planks, an inch in thickness, which were
taken from the old Caledonian forest, and the three-
inch long wooden pins with which the slates were
fixed, are still in preservation.

The first quarries were worked below high-water
mark. Wedges of hard wood were driven into the
cracks and seams of the slate strata at low tide,
so that when the high tide came in and covered
them the wood might swell and split the rock.
Indeed, this was the ancient Eastern way of quarry-
ing the great stones used in Egypt and at Baalbec.
The workers drove great wedges of wood between
the stones of the quarry and poured water on them,
and the water swelled them until they split the rock.
But at Easdale, in order to keep those tidal quarry-
holes dry, the workmen had to dig a trench from
the working place to the lowest tide mark that
the water might run out.

In the Old Statistical Account (1795) we find that
wages for day labourers, or feuars as they were
called, varied from 9*d*. or 10*d*. a day throughout the
year. Three hundred men were then employed;
5,000,000 slates were quarried annually : and the
quarriers themselves were paid 10*s*., 12*s*., or 15*s*.
per thousand slates, in proportion to the difficulty
of working.

To-day the quarries are still active, after all
these centuries. The result is that Easdale has kept
its population, while other districts of the Highlands,
through the failure of local industries, like kelp or
marble or fishing, have been almost altogether
depopulated.

Seil is an island bounded on every side by
Sounds. On the north-east there is Clachan Sound,
on the east there is the Sound of Seil, on the west
there is Easdale Sound, and on the south there is
Cuan Sound. I went down the road through the
island to Cuan Sound, where there is a ferry across
the narrow strait to the Island of Luing. Here
there are a few cottages, and the old local hospital.
The tide runs very swiftly through Cuan Sound,
which is so truly described by its name, the " narrow
sea." From the shores of Cuan Sound, looking
north-west, there is a glorious view across the
Firth of Lorne to the mountains of Mull. The day

was so clear that it was easy to notice with the naked eye a great landslide of rock on the bastion cliffs of that island. It is rightly called Mull of the Mountains, and each of them has its appropriate name. Dun na Ghaoithe is the Hill of the Winds; Sgurr Dearg the Red Hill; Ben Taladh the Mount of Allurement; Ben Creach the Clam Shell Hill; Ben Buie the Yellow Hill; and mighty Ben More lords it over them all.

It was on the way back from Cuan that the real point of the day's pilgrimage was reached, at the old churchyard of Kilbrandon, on the east side of the road, not far from the little village of Balvicar. The site of Kilbrandon old church, with its graveyard, was well chosen. It stands on the summit of a little green hill which commands a fine view on every side. In the graveyard which is still used, there is one scrap of the ancient church left, a mere vault or low arch. St. Brendan was the sailor saint of the early Celtic Church who sailed from Ireland and became the Apostle of the Isles. Indeed, the " Pilgrimage of St. Brendan " has been called the Christian Odyssey. In the Aberdeen Breviary we read, " St. Brendan having sailed to the west of Scotland fixed his residence on the top of a hill, whose base stretched into the sea, on the spot known as Sedes Brendani, where only one

ISLE OF SCARBA FROM SEIL

[To face page 118

ship could enter." One would like to imagine
that this hill might be the Hill of Brendan, and
that the narrow stream under Clachan Bridge was
the channel where only one boat could enter.
There are many old and interesting stones of Celtic
design near the ruined vault, but most of them
are under the turf to-day, reminding one of the
wise words of Sir Thomas Browne—" Large are
the treasures of oblivion; much more is buried
in silence than is recorded."

Here, almost covered with grass, is a flat stone.
By removing the grass the name and date are clear :
" Here lyes Margaret Campbell, spous to Robert
Grant of Branchell, who died at Obane, the ninth
of September, 1681." Brenchoille is on Lochfyne
side, and Oban is the " Little Bay " on the Island
of Seil. I tell the tragic story of this one stone
as an example of the history that lies behind many
of these ancient grave slabs. Robert Grant was
factor to Lord Neil Campbell of Ardmaddy, who
sent him to collect the rents in Islay. When the
factor was returning, the Macleans of Duart seized
him in the Sound of Luing, and carried him off
to Duart Castle in Mull. For there was bad blood
between Lord Neil and Duart. When he heard
the news Lord Neil asked his friend MacDougal
of Dunolly to go and bargain for Grant's release.

He paid a visit to Maclean. But Duart suspected what he had come about and sent word secretly to his men to behead Grant. Then, with the utmost politeness, he asked MacDougal to postpone discussing business until he had refreshed himself. After the feast was over Dunolly asked Duart to release the factor. " Take his body, if you like," answered Duart with a malicious smile, " it is lying ready in the courtyard. But I keep the head." MacDougal, seeing how things were, took up the headless body, and the dust of it lies here under this stone to-day.

But the object I came here to find was the Chin of Macmarquis. And there it is : a curiously rounded stone, with a projecting base very like a human chin, standing loosely on the top of the flat family tombstone of the Maclachlans, which is raised on four stone pillars. The Chin stone is about a foot high, and you can lift it quite easily, revealing the unweathered mark which lying there on the flat gravestone for so long a time has made. It is locally known as Smig mhic Mharcuis, that is, the Chin of Macmarquis. There is a point of land at the north end of the Sound of Easdale called Rudha mhic Mharcuis, so he must have been a local hero. The strange thing about this stone is that it is believed to be able to turn on its own axis. When a new-made grave has been filled in, the Chin is always found next morning pointing to it; and when the next burial takes place the Chin, in a similar way, is found pointing to the new grave. So has it been for generations. Yet no one has ever been caught, night or day, turning the stone. Stranger still, the stone has often disappeared for a little time, lifted, if you like; but it has invariably reappeared. No one, however, has ever been caught lifting it or bringing it back.

The late Dr. Patrick H. Gillies, who was for many years in the district and loved it, once tested the truth of the story. His monument stands in a corner of the churchyard. He took the Chin home with him and locked it securely in his cellar. Next morning he unlocked the door, and made to lift the Chin. But, it was gone! When he went to the churchyard to look for it, there it was standing on the flat tombstone as usual.

So the Chin of Macmarquis is safe. For in the Highlands it is as true to-day as it was in Israel twenty centuries ago: " Cursed is he that removeth his neighbour's landmark." Forbye all that, there are some things which even the wisest do not understand.

I

XIV

OLD ARGYLL:
ITS GREY MEMORIALS

As I came down the road on the east side of Loch Awe towards Ford there was nothing new to see or hear. Each sight and sound was as old as the world itself. Yet when April comes there is nothing old or stale about the immortal ritual of the spring. The day blazed with beauty. A blue-white sky; brilliant sunshine; a touch of north in the wind to intensify visibility; the loch one sheet of sapphire; on the hills masses of purple where the bare birches grow; the delicate green mist of the bursting larches; and the duller green of the pines. And for music, whaups gurling on the moors; noisy oyster-catchers *tu-leeping* along the shores; and the peesweeps adding their double note of joy on the meadow. Timeless sights and sounds, the oldest yet the newest in the world, the colour and music of the spring which many an exiled Scot would give anything to see and hear.

I stepped aside to visit the ruins of Fincharn Castle, cocked defiant on the shore. As I climbed the rock I thought of Gillascop MacGilchrist, who got the lands of Fincharn from Alexander III; and of a certain Mac Mhic Ian, a later owner of the castle, who possessed the *droit du seigneur*. This Mac Mhic Ian attended the wedding feast of the daughter of a tenant, and was prepared to claim his right. The bridegroom was absent from the feast, which had just begun, when word was brought that the castle was on fire. Mac Mhic Ian hastened home to find the castle given over to flames, and on the meadow below it the bridegroom waiting for him, sword in hand. The fight began, and soon Mac Mhic Ian lay dead in the light of the blazing keep. Old days, sad days, days of love and hate, when men in the full strength of life played with death, and the clash of the claymore was heard on the very doorsteps of home. Centuries come and go, but memories cling like lichen on many a crumbling wall.

Then I turned up the old hill-road which was once a highway between Fincharn on Loch Awe and Crarae on Loch Fyne. To-day the first part of it is well defined, with a firm causey foundation; I even noticed motor tyre marks for a hundred

yards or so. On a little tree-clad hillock on the left stands the ruined kirk of Kilneuair. There is a curious tradition which connects this church on Loch Awe with the church of Kilevin, at Crarae, on Loch Fyne. Both were dedicated to St. Eoghan. The stones of Kilevin Church are said to have been carried over this road from Crarae for twelve miles by a long line of men, who stood close to one another and handed on each stone, until the last one was built into the walls of Kilneuair Church at Loch Awe.

Soft-padding reivers and sandalled monks must often have travelled this way. But to-day the kirk at Kilneuair is in ruins, and the graveyard a haunted place. It was here that the tailor of Ford defied the local ghost by wagering that he would make a pair of trews in the churchyard at midnight without fear. Despite this defiance, the ghost came out of a grave, made a grab at the tailor with a hairy grey hand, and said : " I am hungry, and will get you with this ! " The trews were found next morning unfinished, but the tailor was never seen again.

Strange to say, a friend has just sent to me a photograph of the stone doorway, and on the third stone from the ground there are the distinct marks of five finger tips and the palm of the right hand !

I missed this mark of the grey hand, but I found

daffodils growing on the grassy floor; a worn inscription on the lintel of the door; a large square font-like stone with a drain-hole in it standing within the ruin; two aumbries—one on the east wall, and the other on the north; two doors on the south; an older course of large, square stones in the lower walls, and a newer course of smaller stones in the upper walls. There are two carved Celtic stones lying on the grass at the south-east corner of the ruin, and one sword stone between the doors. The names on the more modern tombstones were McPhedran, Paul, Macdonald, Gillies, and Crawford; but I saw no Campbell stones, although the Campbells were for a time lords of Fincharn.

There is a curious ruined chapel-like building west of the church, with pointed windows filled in. I took it for a burial vault but, inside or out, I could find no trace of an inscription.

From Ford you can either take the quiet old road to Kilmichael Glassary, passing Kirnan—where Thomas Campbell wrote his "Lines on visiting a scene in Argyllshire," and where to-day there is one of the finest rock gardens in the Kingdom—or you can take the road past Loch Ederline, and so join the main road to Oban a mile or two above Kilmartin. Just before you come to the junction of these roads your eye will be drawn to a great castle standing on a height across the valley. That is Carnassary Castle, and here I must begin my sincere tribute to the authorities who see to the preservation of our ancient and historical nomuments for all they have done in this district to save the priceless memorials of the past.

Until quite recently Carnassary Castle was an ivy-covered ruin, so buried among trees that passers-by on the road far below could scarcely see it. Now some of the trees have been cut down, the walls stripped of the mischievous ivy, and the fine stone-work saved from further decay. For the first time you can get an adequate idea of this imposing building.

I walked up the hillside and found entrance through a seemly little gate, with a stone path, and a sweep of green lawn surrounding most of the building. There is now revealed a fine bit of sculptured tracery above the door. I had forgotten to ask at the cottage on the roadside for the key, so I had to scramble through a window to get on to the ground floor. Here I found a fine old well, beautifully restored. I then explored the whole ruin from the great hall to the topmost

THE KILMARTIN VALLEY

[To face page 126

turret. From the giddy height there is a magnificent view.

The present castle was built on the site of an older one by *An Carsalach Mhor*—the Big Carswell —that is, John Carswell, who was appointed by Queen Mary to the Bishopric of Argyll, a post to which he was never consecrated. Indeed, he was censured by the General Assembly. The Big Cleric then retired to his castle of Carnassary and employed his leisure in making a scholarly translation of John Knox's Liturgy from English into Gaelic. This was the first book to be printed in Gaelic. Three copies of this rare book exist, one of them in the library of Edinburgh University. A single sentence from the preface will suffice to establish the modesty and devotion of this scholarly man :

> If I saw any man of the Gael, of Alban, or Eirind, that should undertake, in aid of the Church of God, to translate this book into the Gaelic language, in which men could understand it, it would be very grateful to me, and I would not undertake the work ; but since none such has been found, or if there be, I do not know him, who will undertake it out of love to God and to the Church, with more ability than my means and my power can bring to it, I hope that God will aid me in my defects and ignorance.

I came down from the castle feeling very grateful for the restoration of this monument to *An Carsalach Mhor*. But my gratitude was to be greatly increased before my week in Knapdale was over.

The carved stones of Kilmartin are well cared for. The district round Carnassary, Poltalloch, Duntroon, and Dunadd is famous for its standing stones, its chambered cairns, and its forts. One such cairn near Kilmartin has been restored by the same authorities.

I made my usual visits down Loch Sween to Kilmory Knap and Keills. Here I found delightful surprises. When I came near Castle Sween—that great bluff citadel of stone standing on its rock by the shore—I saw that it also had been stripped of its heavy masses of ivy, and when I got down to the castle itself I found that all had been restored. I will not weary the reader with historical details or descriptions. It is enough to know that Castle Sween was one of the battle centres of the Lordship of the Isles. The very name of the castle makes us think of a certain Swen Ruoidh, Thane of Glassary and Knapdale, who lived at the castle in the thirteenth century.

In that old book of Gaelic Literature, "The Book of the Dean of Lismore," there are two poems which refer to Castle Sween. One is by Eafric McCorqudale, who seems to have been the wife of the last McNeil of Castle Sween. If any woman knew what the sorrows of war meant it was the wife of a fighting islesman. So she writes her lament :

> Among our women there is no joy,
> Our men no pleasure have in sport ;
> Just like the winds when it is calm
> So without music is Dun Sween.
> See the palace of a generous race,
> Vengeance is taken on Clan Neil,
> Broken my heart is in my breast ;
> And so 'twill be until I die.

The other poem is by a blind Irish bard, Arthur MacCurkich, who describes an attack by the Irish MacSweenys on the Castle. His words make a perfect saga of war :

> The assembled fleet at Castle Sween,
> Pleasant tidings at Innisfail.
>
>   *   *   *   *
>
> Tall men did manage the ship,
>
>   *   *   *   *
>
> A slashing, vigorous noble band.
>
>   *   *   *   *
>
> Who is he provides this fleet,
> At Castle Sween of many hills ?
> A vigorous man who fears no blast,
> His masts upraised, seeking his right,
> John McSween, sail thou the ship
> On the ocean's fierce topped back.
>
>   *   *   *   *

Then did we fight at Castle Sween.
*　　　*　　　*　　　*
Every limb endowed with strength,
We pierced the bodies of our foes,
Just as a serpent fiercely wounds.
We raised the cry of the great McSween.

But it was when I came to Kilmory Knap that my heart swelled with pride at the work of restoration that has been done there. Only one who loves those beautiful old Celtic stones, with their ancient carved patterns, and knows each one apart, can understand what it was to come on this roofless ruin of a church, with its precious fragments so finely preserved. A year or two ago the stones were lying among the grass, within the church, exposed to the weather, and greatly defaced by a countless number of careless visitors who walked continually over them with hob-nailed shoes. Indeed, the exquisite tracery has been very much obliterated since James Drummond made his exact drawings of them in 1866. Many a time have I called attention to the alarming wastage of this unique form of Celtic art.

But now the little churchyard is all cleaned up and well kept. The ruined walls have been pointed and made secure. A glass roof covers the entire building. The grass-grown floor is gone, and a seemly cement one has been substituted. In the middle of this floor there is a square, stepped

LOCH SWEEN

[To face page 130]

socket for a cross which puzzled me, for it is quite
new. Leaning up against the walls are about thirty
slabs, all cleaned of moss and earth, with their lovely
carvings now revealed in a good light. I went round
them all. And then—like a father who knows all
his children and misses one that is absent—I mur-
mured, " But where is the broken slab with the
little font-like hollow at the foot of the carving? "
No wonder I missed this stone, for Drummond
wrote of it seventy years ago : " The most curious
is a fragment richly decorated with scroll work,
but having one end scooped out like a holy water
stoup." I looked everywhere and could not find it.
But on returning to Edinburgh I found out that
the other half of this cross shaft had been discovered by the reverent restorer. The two halves
are now being properly joined up, and are being
sent back, that this finely united shaft of a cross
may be erected in the empty cross socket which I
puzzled over. So efficiently is this work of restoration being planned and carried out. Now, the
treasures of Kilmory Knap are permanently secured,
and the place is an object lesson on what might be
done elsewhere if enough money were forthcoming.

That led me to revisit Keills, on the other side
of Loch Sween. Here all lies derelict as of old.

I may be pardoned if I repeat a sentence which I wrote years ago about Keills :

It hurts the heart to see nothing but weeds, nettles, and thistles in this sacred enclosure, and the stones sadly weathered since the drawings and rubbings in the books mentioned were taken, over fifty years ago. It makes me tremble to think what they will be like in another fifty years if no loving hand preserves them.

Now my heart is at rest. For what has already been done at Kilmory Knap will shortly be done at Keills. At Keills, James Drummond sketched nine beautiful stones in 1866. I wonder if the restorers will find them all at Keills to-day !

XV

THE SINGLE-HANDED CHANTER: A TALE OF SLASHED FINGERS

I NEVER look at this home-made Single-handed Chanter[1] but I think of the legend of Slashed Fingers.

It was found in a peat bog in the Glen of Gloomy Memories, near the ruins of the old Chief's house. A mere relic now, but it is of supreme interest to all pipers.

I fell heir to the chanter in this way. The old doctor was a Macdonald of Glencoe. He got the chanter in a gift from his cousin in the Glen, Duncan McInnes. In a letter which accompanied the gift, and which lies before me as I write, McInnes states that the chanter was found by D. Aitchison, the keeper, when he was digging in the bog. As I got the Chanter and the letter direct from the doctor, there can be no doubt of the authenticity of the curious little *feadan* or chanter.

As all pipers know, the ordinary bagpipe chanter has seven finger holes on the front of it, and one

[1] *Bagpipe Chanter.*—The finger pipe, with eight holes in it, on which the melody is played with both hands.

thumb hole on the back. It takes a pair of strong hands, both thumbs, and all fingers but the little one on the left hand to hold and play the pipes. But what must the difficulty have been for a piper who, after losing one hand, was yet so fiercely in love with piping that he had to make himself a rough chanter out of a bit of wood! It would only require a thumb hole behind, and four finger holes in front. Even then, to hold it while playing, the piper must have rested the foot of his stumpy makeshift on the front of his chest.

I know not what kind of wood it is made of. But it has been perfectly preserved in a peat bog from time immemorial. It is ten and a half inches long by one and a quarter inches broad. It has a roughly shaped tapering top, with a groove cut round it for a string to hold the chanter reed in place. From end to end the core has been burned out with some red hot instrument. The five finger holes, like the core, are still charred black with the burning. But that is not wonderful, for there is no better preservative than peat.

The old doctor sent it to me first on loan, and asked me to have it examined by the antiquarian experts in Edinburgh. After taking it to the Museum I exhibited it before the Scottish Pipers' Society. But nowhere could I find anyone who

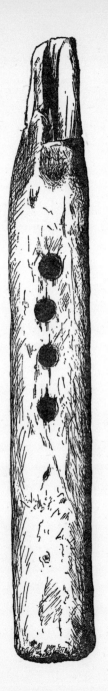

GLE-HANDED.
NTER:
----
nd in a peat
by the Keeper
itchison when
ging near the
ns of the Chiefs
use at
nlichnamue
ncoe. 1924.

wn to scale
actual size.

Extract from letter sent
by Duncan Macinnes of
26 Carnoch-: Glencoe: on
July 14. 1924:- To D.Y. D.
Macdonald of Laggan-
in whose possession it
now is:-

" I herewith enclose what
resembles a Chanter, which
was found in a peat bog
by the Keeper D. Aitchison
near the ruins of the Chief's
House at Glenlichnamue.
Glencoe."

JMS.
Aug: 15th

had ever seen anything like it. So I returned it to my old friend, whose it was by the inalienable right of possession, and he kept it until his death.

I have written elsewhere[1] an account of the splendid self-sacrifice and bravery of the doctor, who was awarded the Carnegie Medal for Valour in saving life at the risk of his own. After his death, to my surprise and delight, his widow sent me the Single Handed Chanter with a note telling me that this curious old relic was a legacy from her husband. So it rests with me, in safe keeping, to-day.

Despite the somewhat broken mouthpiece which is meant to hold the reed, I have on more than one occasion fitted a practice chanter reed in it and succeeded in bringing some notes from it. But when it last sounded a note who can tell?

Why did it ever happen that a piper should have only one hand? That question is the mystery which brings me to the old story of Slashed Fingers. And a bloody tale it is, with fine piping in it, bitter jealousy, and a stepmother's fearful revenge. All lovers of Neil Munro's writings will find it in his *Red Hand*. There, it is elaborated in his own Gaelic way which no mere outsider has ever been able to imitate. I always intended to send him the single-handed chanter for his comment, as a pos-

[1] See " *The Land of Locheil,*" chap. 20.

sible illustration of the legend. But, alas, death
rebukes many a tardy intention. The story may
be briefly told as follows :

There was at some time or other before now,
a namely piper called Duncan Dall, and as his
name indicates he was blind. None in the glen
or by the lochside could match his skill when he
threw the drones over his shoulder, filled the bag,
and brought notes of dool or merriment from the
deeps of time. Pipers are born to the gallantry
of their art. When to the art is added blindness,
a man is doubly endowed with insight into the
meaning that lies behind the notes of a *piobaireachd*.
When, however, to skill and blindness is added a
piper's inveterate jealousy, then the fire of mischief is kindled.

This Donald Dall had a son by his first wife,
and the boy Angus Og inherited the gift from his
blind father, but with something added to it. So
the father-wise man sent the son to Boreraig, the
MacCrimmon's College of Piping in Skye, where
a lad with the gift could learn all that was to be
known of fine piping. Yonder, by Dunvegan
Loch, night and morning, year in, year out, Angus
Og paced the green turf of MacCrimmon's parade
ground on the hoe above the sea, practising the
piobaireachd—for nothing but the classic music of

K

the *piob mhor* was allowed by the Prince of Pipers. Then a day came when the master player said to his pupil : " Go home, Angus Og—for I can teach you no more." So he returned to his father's home.

Very soon they had a contest. The blind old man played first, and he played well. But when he laid down the pipes the son in the foolish pride of his youth took up his set and said with a smile, " Father, you play not so ill for a man who is old and blind. But here is the MacCrimmon way."

Then Angus Og threw the drones over his shoulder and played.

The old man did not see the smile of pity on his son's face, but old Annapla did, and hatred leapt in her step-heart like a flame. So, when the piping was over, she watched with bitterness the chagrin of the old man who had been put to shame. Had not Angus Og stricken his father as surely as if he had dirked him ?

That night, when Angus Og had returned to the hut on the shore, Annapla whispered poisoned words in the ear of Duncan Dall, and before the night was out the old man was cursing his son. A storm came up from the sea, and long past midnight the old woman was struggling against the wind as she made her way down to the hut where Angus Og was sleeping. Pushing open the door,

she crept into the bothy, and there she saw Angus
Og lying by the light of the peat fire, sound asleep,
with his right hand thrust out from the blanket,
as helpless as a child. Annapla stamped out the
peat fire. She stood in the darkness and drew
from under her plaid the little black knife of
Duncan Dall. Stooping down stealthily she felt
for the sleeper's hand. Then—she struck! With
a yell of pain Angus Og leaped out of his dreams.
But there was no one in the dark hut to hear his
anguish.

.   .   .   .   .

That is the legend of the Slashed Fingers.
Gruesome enough. But it is a possible commen-
tary on the Single-Handed Chanter and why any
piper in the sad old days should fashion this
strange instrument out of a bit of wood.

XVI

APRIL ORCHESTRA : MUSIC IN THE GLEN

LISTENING to nature is like listening to orchestral music—it takes a lifetime to learn, and even then the half has not been told. If you would become acquainted with the myriad notes in the music of nature and the instruments that make them, you must learn to watch, to listen, and to be patient in utter solitude. Then, you will gradually accumulate a first-hand knowledge which does not depend on books and which no man can gainsay. One of the very first things you will learn is that the music of nature is not only made up of sounds, for there is a music in colour, just as there is a colour in music.

If only I could reproduce with exactitude some of the sights and sounds of nature in the glen this April day ! Blue skies that are deeper and more liquid than any on earth : great white clouds floating in them more dazzling than any snow : and purple shadows creeping over the hills. Little birches not yet in bud, which run along the hillside like whiffs of grey mist that is all the more diaphanous because the sun is shining through millions of twigs. Larches with their tender green tassels already out-matching the birches. Every shade of brown, grey, yellow, and black on the hills and on their rocky ramparts, such as you can never see in the green effulgence of summer. The blue-green of the Scots firs and long bare stretches of benty grass.

The river is very low to-day in its deep defile of rocks. But I have seen it racing down in such terrific spate that the sound of it was like the roaring of a lion let loose, and its debris-laden waters were as tawny as the lion's mane. Indeed, the wild beast was so fierce that it seemed unsafe to go near it.

But the bird music of April makes the finest of all the notes in the springtide symphony. I do not mean the almost overpowering and never-ending chorus of bird music that wakens so many of us at dawn, when it is almost impossible to pick out the individual notes of certain birds, so unified is the sound of all the performers. Rather do I mean the many different sounds of nature which I can hear in the glen to-day. On the moors of Scotland there is nothing in April to equal the heart-stirring call of the whaup, that great, grey, long-beaked bird which is beloved of every wandering Scot. First comes the slow, ascending whistle

at the beginning of the call, repeated again and
again, like a quiet prelude before an outburst of
music ; then the sudden rapture of the love thrill
which fills the glen with a gurl of passion that
is too intense to last long : until the long, low
notes come again, only to die away like the
wail of a lost spirit.   Were I an exiled Scot in a
foreign land, the one thing for which I would yearn
when April comes would be the cry of the whaup :

> "The whaup's wild cry on the breeze blawn by,
>   Like a wanderin' word frae hame."

But there are other songsters at work in the
orchestra.   In the woods by the river the finches
are making happy music with no hint of sadness
in it.   To this the willow warblers add their song.
with just an extra dribble of notes in the final
phrasing—a falling cadence at the end which has
a very subtle effect on the listener.   Sitting here
in this Scots glen, listening to the willow warblers,
my memory flies to a magic night of Ramadan in
Damascus, years ago, where for the first time I
heard an Arab woman singing a song of the
desert in the blue dusk ; for, in the Arab music
as in the willow warbler's song, there is this same
tumble of notes at the close which haunts you
with a certain sense of regret.

Across the river a great tit is singing. This bird is commonly called the " Musical Saw," because its double note is so like the sound of a wood saw. Again I am reminded that this double note is reproduced in one of the movements of Tchaikovsky's Fifth Symphony in E minor. He composed the symphony in the year 1888 while he was staying in his new country house at Frolovskoe, near Klin, and he tells us how much he enjoyed the little garden on the edge of the forest, with the wide outlook beyond it over the homely landscape of Central Russia. Writing to his friend, von Meck, to whom he dedicated the Fourth Symphony, he says :

> I cannot tell you what a pleasure it has been to watch my flowers grow. . . . When I am quite old and past composing, I shall devote myself to growing flowers. Meanwhile, I have been working with good results, for half the Symphony is now orchestrated.

In these happy circumstances, among the flowers and the trees, Tchaikovsky must have heard and noted the double note of the " Musical Saw," else he could never have reproduced it so exactly in this particular movement. Indeed, I never hear the Fifth Symphony in the dreary winter time but I listen eagerly for this passage, for it makes me realise that spring is near.

But there are many other sounds to-day in the spring orchestra. Peesweeps calling on the flat fields by the river : lambs bleating everywhere : the yellow-hammer on a hedgerow calling for the first time for " a little bit of bread and no cheese " : a pheasant sending its hollow and raucous *kuk-kuk* through the home woods : and a little brown squirrel adding its own tiny notes to the music as it runs up a tree trunk and peers down on the intruder with a twinkle of mischief in its eye. I have sat in a Ross-shire wood, as silent and as still as a stone, listening to the converse of several squirrels in the trees above me : and once on an April day in Rannoch I stood looking up a pine trunk at a squirrel which crept gradually down, looked right into my eyes, and spoke to me in two notes—*quince-quince*—which is the sound in words as nearly as I can reproduce it. So, even a squirrel can add its little note to the spring orchestra, like the double pizzicato of a violin string.

But there is another squirrel note which is often heard. Two squirrels at this moment are making acrobatic excursions up the trees, and jumping like trapeze artists from branch to branch. They make strange little *knock-knock* sounds, like castanets with their well-shod feet, every time they run up and down the trunks. When they pause to nibble at the bark their tails are laid forward along their backs. When climbing a branch with jerky scoots, their tails keep twitching up and down. When running on the grass or branch their tails stick straight behind. *Knock-knock* go the squirrels, and when I rise they disappear, leaving me to listen to a cushat dove crooning among the larches across the river near Woodend, and somewhere in the same direction the inevitable owl, dovering in a tree, seemed to have mistaken high noon for slumberous night. *Knock-knock* go the squirrels again, and then they disappear in the thick wood. So the castanets in the orchestra are silent.

A little further up the glen, the oriflamme of a roe-deer appears suddenly among the trees. The oriflamme was originally the name given to the sacred silk banner of St. Denis which used to be given by the Abbot to the early French kings when they were starting out for a war. Then it came to mean any blaze of colour or bright object which attracted attention. It is now used for the snow-white rump of a roe-deer. Yonder it glows like a white flame in the wood. When it disappeared, I looked at the steep screes of Creag Mhor and remembered that far up in that forest the great stags are putting forth their new horns at this very moment : for, when the bracken begins to send up the first crozier-like curls of green, the stags begin to grow their new antlers. The tender points of these, in their first growth, are so soft and vulnerable that, if broken, the stag may bleed to death ; but six months after this, when the velvet is off the horns, the antlers will be as hard as iron, and will crown many a magnificent head with an incomparable set of war weapons.

In the lower reaches of the river by Peter's Pool the noisy oyster-catchers—those swift-flying, black-and-white darts of energy—are calling continually *tu-leep*, *tu-leep*. They send their cheerful cries in at the open window to awake us at the dawn, and they fill the darkening night with the same boisterous call, for they never seem to sleep. The old Celts called the oyster-catcher " St. Bride's Bird," and when it sent its happy call over the waves in the evening the isles folk said that Bride was in laughter.

In the afternoon a blackbird always sings high up on a tree near the salmon ladders. It has a round, fluted song which never rises very high and never falls very low, but it contains the richest of all the notes in bird music. Its companion is the thrush, which has a far larger range of song, and far more rapture in its singing. The thrush's song may be the lover's outburst; but the blackbird's song is love at its best. The first rapture has died down, and love is transformed into that deep and even happiness which is never-ending.

XVII

FORTINGALL: THE HEART OF PERTHSHIRE

SOME write about places after a flying visit to them. Others write about them because they have found in them a home. Fortingall was my postal address for seven summers; and, as with Jacob and his Rachel, the seven years seemed but a few days, because of the love which I conceived for this incomparable district. Rannoch to the north; Glenlyon to the west; Strathtay to the east; Ben Lawers and the loch to the south, with Fortingall at the centre of the circle: where in all Scotland could a lover find a land of bens and glens and heroes more glamorous than this? Add to all that, the history, literature, and legendry of the Celts seethe round Fortingall. The village is one of the most beautiful in Scotland, and, for me at least, the dearest spot of all is an old white house beaking in the sun, above the sparkling waters of Peter's Pool, on one of the finest salmon rivers in Scotland.

" God gave all men all earth to love,
   But since our hearts are small,
Ordained for each one spot should prove
   Beloved over all."

The quiet valley which runs for four miles from
Coshieville to the Bridge of Lyon is the natural
gateway of Glenlyon. The statue of General
David Stewart of Garth, which stands by the roadside near Coshieville, makes a fine introduction
to our day's stravaig; for he wrote about the history of the Highlands and the Highland regi-
ments; and his *Sketches* is a classic. If, however,
you would visit the early home of the Stewarts
of Garth and Drumcharry, you must walk up the
Rannoch road for a mile or two, and high up
on the west side of the Keltney burn you will
come on the ruins of that grim old keep Garth
Castle, which was once a stronghold of the
notorious Wolf of Badenoch —"the curst whelp's
castle."

The quiet fertile strath of Garth is bounded
on the south by the heathery slopes of Drummond Hill and on the north by the outlying spurs
of the Glenlyon mountains. The river here runs
peacefully by the roadside, past the woodlands of
the modern Garth House, and just across the swing
bridge you will find the ancient beech avenue which
leads to Duneaves House—a natural cathedral

nave of tall pillared tree trunks, arched over
with innumerable branches and laid with a carpet
of fine old turf. From this road on the south
side of the river Lyon you get the best view of
Fortingall village, sleeping in the sun along the
hill-foots, and guarded by the great massif of
Creag Mhor. An avenue of old trees to-day;
but, if you have the gift and walk down it at high
noon when the sun is sweltering and the air is still,
it becomes a promenade of ghosts. Then you will
hear the clansmen peching as they run with targe
and claymore to the fight, for the fiery cross has
just gone by, and brave women are looking after
them, with their children clinging to their skirts
gulping down their fears.

It would take too long to tell the history of this
valley, which in olden times was a corridor of war.
You get the key to the ancient warfare if you
climb to the top of the little green hill of Dungeal,
behind Balnacraig. There you will find the ruins
of a very old British fort, where a Caledonian chief
once lived and from his eyrie commanded the
whole approaches of the valley. As you sit on
the stones enjoying the view, you can imagine
all the clash and clang of primitive warfare that
surged up and down the valley. You can see
below you many pagan relics which remind you

of the dark age before the Celtic saints arrived. Here on the slope of a hillock to the east of the fort is a cup-marked stone. Down on the flat field near the village are the remains of two stone circles. On the level space further on where the so-called Roman Camp stands, you will find a large, oblong boulder lying on a slight eminence among the broom bushes with a number of cups on it. On the Fearnan road there is a huge boulder called the *Clach an Tuirc*, or Boar Stone, with more cups on it. Even in the enclosure of Sir Donald Currie's burial-place at Fortingall Church there stands an upright stone covered with cups. There are many more in the neighbourhood. Whether these cup-marked stones were used for pagan altars of sacrifice, or for sun worship, or for astronomical purposes, we shall never know. At least we do know that when the Celtic saints arrived they often used a centre of pagan worship for the site of their little Christian cell, sometimes even imposing a cross and font on the cup-marked stone, thus visibly grafting the new religion on to the old paganism.

A handful of grey stones on the moor or among the broom bushes : but when you finger the cup marks you have only to look over your shoulder, and there are the Druid priests and the wild men from the hills, and strange incantations coming down the wind that blows about the broom bushes, whose dry pods crackle in the August heat like the sound of sacrificial flames.

The saints came to Fortingall down Glenlyon from the west and far Iona in the sixth and seventh centuries. St. Adamnan, who was one of Columba's successors, and his biographer, often passed this way. He has left many traces up and down the glen, as I have pointed out elsewhere.[1] The Churchyard of St. Ciaran stood somewhere on the south side of the river, and behind the wall on the road (just before it dips down to Fearnan) you will find the old baptismal font of the saint with this inscription on a metal plate : " The Baptismal Font of the Church dedicated to Saint Ciaran, which stood near this spot."

But Cedd was the real patron saint of Fortingall. When Aidan went from Iona to Lindisfarne he brought back to Scotland two Anglo-Saxon converts, the brothers Cedd and Chad. They came north to Iona for further instruction in the faith. On their way back to Northumbria they settled for a time at Fortingall, for their father-in-God, Aidan, was the patron saint of the neighbouring parish of Inchaidan, which is now called Kenmore.

[1] " *The Road to Rannoch*," chap. 8.

Cedd built a church at Fortingall and Chad another
at Logierait. Indeed, there is a tradition that a
slab on the roadside is the grave of St. Cedd, and
he is still commemorated by two place-names
at Fortingall—one, *Dail-math-Choede*, the Field
of Cedd; the other, *Feil-math-Choede*, the Fair of
Cedd, which was held on 20th August. After
that St. Cedd became Bishop of London, and St.
Chad Bishop of Lichfield. One of the most
precious treasures of Lichfield Cathedral is " The
Gospels of St. Chad."

The church at the Kirkton of Fortingall is well
worth a visit. The old parish church, the hotel,
and the picturesque thatched cottages in the village were all beautifully restored by Sir Donald
Currie when he bought the estates of Garth and
Glenlyon. In the church there is preserved, within
a niche of the stone wall behind the pulpit, one
of the few remaining Celtic bells of Scotland, dating,
it is said, from the seventh century. It is very
properly locked up behind an open grill of wrought-
iron work. The metal of the bell was analysed
by the late Mr. W. Ivison Macadam, and was found
to be a mixture of iron, copper, and tin. Another
Celtic bell of similar type was discovered in 1870
between the wall and the eaves of an old cartshed
on the farm of Balnahanait, in Glenlyon; it was

L

very thin and eaten with rust, the handle nearly gone. Still another Celtic bell I have seen in the manse of Innerwick in the glen. It used to stand in a niche of the churchyard wall at Kerrowmore, or Cladh Bhrennu, as the old cemetery was called. That three ancient bells have been found in the neighbourhood is a unique circumstance, and a proof of how strong the Celtic Church was in the district.

In Fortingall churchyard there stands the oldest yew tree in Scotland. To support that daring statement I have only to refer to the report made by the late Sir Robert Christison about 1870, when, after a very careful examination, he declared it to be about 3000 years old. In 1769 Pennant visited Colonel Campbell of Glenlyon, and found that, in spite of being then greatly decayed, it measured 56½ feet in circumference. In 1825 the limbs had fallen apart. It was then surrounded by a wall to preserve it from further harm. When Pennant's report on the tree became known, the famous French botanist, Decandolle, Baron Humboldt, and others testified to the great age of this yew tree. Under its branches lie many of the old Stewarts of Garth.

A still more curious tradition is that Pontius Pilate was born at Fortingall. The story is that the father of Pontius Pilate was sent as an ambas-

sador of peace by Cæsar Augustus to one Metal-
lanus, the local chief, who at that time lived in the
fort at Dungeal. While the ambassador of Rome
was here the future judge of our Lord was born.
I give this strange story as part of the lore of the
place ; but, of course, there is no proof whatever
for it.

The so-called Roman Camp lies to the west of
the village, between the road and the river, not far
from the Bridge of Lyon. It has all the appear-
ance of a Roman Camp, but it has never been
excavated enough to show whether the Romans
penetrated so far to the north-west. Yet we
cannot overlook the words of Haverfield and Macdonald, two of our greatest authorities on the
Romans in Britain :

> We must remember that Roman " Camps " have been
> noted west and north of Inchtuthil—one at Comrie in
> Strathearn, others near Forfar in Strathmore, and one or
> two yet further north, beyond Aberdeen. They are camps,
> not of permanent occupation, but of armies on campaign.
> They are, as yet, wholly unexplored. Till the spade has
> unmasked their secrets it will be rash to stop Agricola at
> Inchtuthil on the Tay.

Just opposite the village, in a field between the
road and the river, there is a round mound on which
there stands an upright stone with a pointed top.
This is the *Clach-na-Marbh* or Stone of the Dead.
On the stone there is the following inscription :

" Here lie victims of the great plague of the 14th century, taken here on a sledge drawn by a white horse, led by an old woman." How vividly one can picture it all. The superstitious people, terrified to touch anyone who died of plague ; the dead lying everywhere unburied ; this old woman, kindly and unafraid, gathering the bodies with her own hands, laying them on the rough sledge, to which she yoked an old white horse ; then, leading the faithful beast across the field, and burying her friends in a rude grave, over which afterwards was piled a heap of stones. When the stars come out over Creag Mhor there is a gleam of a white horse moving about in the gloom near the pillar of the dead, and the call of the night hag sounds like the cailleach keening for those children of sorrow who never seem to keep silence in this world of beauty and care.

Before the Reformation several generations of Macgregors were Vicars of Fortingall. One of them—Dugald the Tonsured—had two sons, James and Duncan. James, like his great-grandfather, was Vicar, and in 1514 was made Dean of Lismore, in Argyll. After his father's death he held the church lands and lived at Tullichmhuilinn, which is now Glenlyon House. He retained the deanery and vicarage till his death in 1551. He

must have been an illustrious cleric, for the Pope
knighted him, and he is still known as Sir James
Macgregor. He and his brother Duncan compiled
The Book of the Dean of Lismore and *The Chronicle
of Fortingall.* This precious manuscript contains
Gaelic poetry taken down from oral recitation
as early as 1512–1526. The Gaelic is written
phonetically, and gives us the exact language which
was in use at that time. Here also are the earliest
Gaelic poems in manuscript attributed to Ossian,
with others by poets of the sixteenth century. It
is therefore the earliest specimen of written Scots
Gaelic, except that contained in the *Book of Deer.*
So the *Book of the Dean of Lismore* gives the lie to
Dr. Johnson's pompous and ignorant assertion
that "the Erse (Gaelic) never was a written language," and that "there is not in the world an
Erse MS. a hundred years old."

As I turn over the leaves of the old book and
try to decipher the quaint wordings on pages
that are now brown with age, I can hear the sennachies reciting their brave stories, and the minstrels
singing their laments which draw the heart-chords
of us who sing them to-day, with the same pains of
love which the harpers drew from the strings
of their clarsachs long ago.

XVIII

THE LAICH O' MORAY—AND THE SANDS OF DEATH

In this year of grace, February yielded us some summer-like days. March proved more or less unkindly. But April will be remembered for its bitter east winds, its hail, sleet, and snow; the deep drifts which blocked the north road; and the floods which swept along some of the Aberdeen-shire roads like roaring rivers. On the 16th day of the month the warm weather returned. But it was too late for us, and we had to be content for ten days with scarifying winds, wintry condi-tions, and hail rattling down the chimney at night to waken us from a troubled sleep.

The Laich of Moray is one of the most beautiful parts of Scotland—that long, flat seaboard which lies to the south of the Moray Firth. Fertile, well wooded and well watered, with rivers that are far famed, from its shores there is a wonderful outgait across the northern sea to the hills of Ross and Cromarty. More than once I set off to explore that lonely ten miles of coast which lies between

Nairn and the Culbin Sands. It is a desolation of dunes, green flats, dark woodlands, and heathery bogs. But it is a perfect paradise for the lover of nature, and the home of all kinds of wild fowl and game.

Charles St. John, the famous naturalist, after looking across the firth from Loch Loy, wrote in his *Wild Sport*:—" Beautiful—surpassing beautiful is the scene which lies before me." St. John resigned his post as a Civil Servant in London in 1833 and came north to devote himself to sport and the study of natural history. He stayed at several places in the north—at Rosehall in Sutherland, at Nairn, and at Elgin. But his real home was at Invererne, near Forres, where the waters of the river Findhorn fall into the great bay of that name.

Another reason for my particular interest in this seaboard is that at the eastern end of it lie the Culbin Sands, beneath which lies buried the ancient Barony of Culbin.

I had intended to explore the shore in a motor boat, and, indeed, had arranged with one of the Nairn fishermen to take me out. But for nearly a fortnight tremendous seas were breaking over the harbour entrance, and mighty rollers thundered along the sands, making an unbroken line of foam

on the edge of the sands which lie to the east of
Nairn.

The perpetual fascination of this shore walk to
me is the Old Bar—a long and very narrow island
of low land which runs parallel to the shore.   At
low water the Bar can be reached across the bare
sand, for it is a little less than half a mile out.
There is one solitary hut or cottage on the Bar for
the accommodation of a salmon fisher in the
season, and one morning I saw a cart and horse
being driven across the sands to that desolate
abode.   On the outer edge of the Bar immense
ridges of gravel and stones have been thrown up
by the pounding seas, and at low tide, when the
sands between the island and the shore are quite
bare, you can hear the low grumble of the breakers
beyond the Bar.   The wet surface of the four
square miles of yellow sand reflects the sky and
clouds with many a gleam of white, opal, amethyst,
and sapphire.   There are, however, many treach-
erous holes in the sand, and during the war a
soldier who was ignorant of the safe way across
was sucked down along with his horse, and both
were drowned, in spite of all that some brave
rescuers attempted.

Apart from the continual grumble of the breakers
far away, the only sounds I heard were the song of

larks above the dunes, whaups gurling above the inland flats, the perpetual calling of seabirds, and the wind in the bent. Loch Loy is a delightful sheet of fresh water lying a little way inland, parallel to the shore, and surrounded by pine trees. Beyond Loch Loy lie the Maviston sands; and beyond them again is the Low Wood or the Forest, and still farther on lie the Culbin Sands. These woods are the home of all kinds of beasts and birds. There is plenty of hard walking across the sedges and bogs and heather tufts. Wild duck fly continually above you, or swim in the waters of the estuary. I flushed some grouse and partridges, in the heather and on the fields. From the dingle of the wood came the hollow call of a cock pheasant. There is a heronry among the Loch Loy trees. This is only April. But later on, in the nesting season, you can scarcely walk on the Bar or in the solitudes of this shore without tramping on a tern's nest.

The view northwards from Loch Loy House is magnificent. Green fields, a dense row of dark trees, and beyond that the sands, the narrow channel of the E'e, as it is called, the low ridge of the Bar, and the wide waters of the Moray Firth. Across the blue sea is the long line of the Ross-shire cliffs, from Rosemarkie to Tarbet Ness, with the entrance to the Cromarty Firth between the North and South Sutors. To live at Loch Loy is to be long-sighted, and no wonder that the dearest of old ladies, at the age of 95, can see in clear weather the lighthouse at Tarbet Ness. The scene is all the more beautiful in April when Ben Wyvis and the Ross-shire hills are dazzling white with snow.

From the gardens behind the house you look southwards across the level land to the ruins of Inshoch Castle, once the seat of the old family of Hay of Loch Loy. The Hays were ardent Covenanters. And just to the south of Inshoch Castle lies Auldearn, where the Great Marquis of Montrose defeated the Covenanting army with a masterly strategy which made the Battle of Auldearn the most brilliant of all Montrose's battles.

But the sandhills which lie on the western side of the great bay of Findhorn are, in one sense, the most unique sandhills in Scotland, for somewhere below the sand there is buried the ancient Barony of Culbin.

The Findhorn is one of the swiftest rivers in Scotland when it comes to a sudden rise, and has been likened to a wild horse that has never been broken in. During the 1829 flood it rose in one place as much as fifty feet. Its source lies 2,800 feet high up among the Monadhliath Mountains, and its entire length is 63 miles from source to sea. When the temperature falls suddenly from winter cold to summer heat, the snow melts so quickly in the upper reaches that the river becomes an uncontrollable torrent by the time it reaches the sea.

That is exactly where our interest in the Old Bar comes in. For in olden times the river rounded the corner at Binsness, turned westwards along the shore towards Nairn, and discharged its waters into the sea at the west end of what we now call the Old Bar. But later on successive floods forced a more direct course to the sea at the bay of Findhorn, and that is what made the Bar the island that it is to-day.

The two deadly dangers, therefore, of the Laich of Moray have always been drifting sand and river floods.

The fair Barony of Culbin was first owned by one called Freskin, who seems to have been a very rich Flemish merchant. William, son of Freskin, Lord of Duffus, was a witness to a charter of 1160 granting the estate of Innes to "Berowald the Fleming," and I find a Hugo de Fresechin a witness to another charter, of date 1150. The Freskins assumed the name of de Moravia, and claimed the vast province of Moray. In the course

of the centuries the heiress Egidia married into
the family of Kinnaird of Kinnaird, and carried the
estates with her. So the Kinnairds succeeded the
Moravias, and for 300 years they owned the Barony
of Culbin. Indeed, in the churchyard of Dyke
there is an old stone with this curious inscription :

Valter : Kinnaird : Elizabeth : Innes : 1613 :
The : Builders : of : this : bed : of : stone :
Ar : laird : and : lady : of : Coolbine :
Qvhilk : Tva : and : Thars : Quhane : Braithe : is :
    gane :
Pleis : God : vil : sleep : This : Bed : Vithin :

Culbin, indeed, was such a beautiful estate in
those days that it was called the Granary of Moray.
Then in the autumn of 1694 a great wind came
out of the west, and a deadly sandstorm overswept
the Barony of Culbin. Just as the fine lava dust
suffocated the inhabitants of Pompeii in the first
century, so the awful clouds of find sand smothered the dwellings of Culbin in the seventeenth
century. The mansion-house, with all its orchards
and lawns, disappeared. Farmhouses and fishermen's houses were sanded over. So suddenly
did the storm arise that a man ploughing fled for
his life, and the plough was found many years
afterwards. The young laird and his wife took
refuge at Earnhill. On the second day there was
a lull in the storm, and the people returned, made

holes in the east end of their houses, and so secured their valuables. Cattle and horses were also retrieved. But that night the sandstorm raged with greater fury than ever, and next morning nothing was visible but a waste of sandhills where once had been a prosperous community.

Needless to say, the laird was ruined. So, in July, 1695, he applied to the Scots Parliament for relief of his land taxes, because " the best two parts of his estate of Culbin, by an unavoidable fatality, was quite ruined and destroyed, occasioned by great and vast heaps of sand." An Act was passed granting him relief, and forbidding for all time, under severe penalties, the pulling of bent juniper and broom. The Act was never repealed.

Of the sixteen farms of Culbin, only one— Earnhill—remains to-day. Then for a hundred years the whole region remained a lost land. But about the year 1798 the old mansion-house reappeared, and remained long enough uncovered to allow the laird to cart away some of the stones for building purposes. Once more the sand laid its silent hand over it, and to-day it lies somewhere at the bottom of the waste of sand hills and dunes. On another occasion an apple tree was laid bare, and actually blossomed. But it too was soon smothered up.

Truly, Culbin is an eerie place to be alone in. You plunge up and down the great slopes ; now hidden from all the world in a valley of death ; now walking along the 100-foot ridge of a great sand hill looking over the trackless wilderness of wind ripples ; but always wrapped about in a silence which is never broken by bird or beast. A mere zephyr will send up a whiff of sand, and a sudden gale will raise dreadful clouds that blind you. Even when an ordinary wind blows up a little hissing dust of powdery particles, a strange fear grips the heart of the lonely loiterer, lest a greater wind should come and enshroud him in a silent death. Distance is elusive, and time seems altogether lost.

The sands of Culbin are also full of flint knives, saws, scrapers, and arrow heads. Anyone who cares to visit the Museum in Queen Street, Edinburgh, will see a countless number of these flints from Culbin. Bronze articles, also, of a later date have been found—rings, rivets, brooches, studs, pins, and an armlet with all kinds of castings, parings, and cuttings. The site of a " bloomery " —that is, a primitive iron furnace—was discovered some years ago. Coins, too, have been found— Roman, French, Flemish, English, and Scots. Indeed, one of the fascinations of wandering about

Culbin is that you never know when you are going to kick up a flint arrow head.

But the natural end of this pilgrimage is at the little village of Findhorn, which stands on the point across the great tidal estuary. Few people realise that there have been three Findhorns. The first stood well out into the Moray Firth in mediæval times. Its exact site, of course, can never now be located, for it was smothered up by sandstorms and washed away by the waters of this wild and shifting seaboard. The second Findhorn, however, is described in the *Survey of Moray*:—" Prior to the year 1701, the town of Findhorn, regularly built, stood upon a pleasant plain a mile north-west from its present situation, and now at the bottom of the sea." One Sunday morning in 1702 both river and sea combined in a great flood, and the little seaport with its quays and warehouses, wharves and jetties, disappeared beneath the angry waters of the North Sea. As I wandered about the present Findhorn village in the rain, I looked about me and wondered how long it would take in the course of the years for the winds and sands and waters of Moray to claim this quaint township as a victim of their deadly storms !

XIX

THE FINEST RIVER IN SCOTLAND:
I—THE UPPER FINDHORN

THE Findhorn, like many a beautiful maiden, is not easily wooed. Over sixty miles long from source to sea, you cannot begin at its head waters and follow a road by its winding side all the way. True, you may travel for some miles along a road that keeps by its banks. But it will suddenly whisk you far away from the river. So in order to explore, you must often find your way along pathless banks, where the river is hidden from any kind of highway, sometimes rushing between steep screes as in The Streens, or plunging through deep-gladed woods as at Glenferness, Conlmony, Relugas, Logie, and Darnaway. Sufficient was it for me this summer to confine my wanderings to the upper reaches of the river, from Coignafearn to Glenferness, with an ideal centre at Tomatin.

The Findhorn rises high up in the Monadh Liath mountains. In seeking the head waters you are

pulled up at old Coignafearn Lodge by a blunt
notice board commanding you to "Stop and
Read." When you do read, you are informed
that the road beyond is private. The road, however, continues for three miles to the new Coignafearn Lodge, and if you still follow the track for
two miles you will come to Dalbeg at the junction
of two streams. Beyond that there has never
been any other house. You are now in the heart
of the Coignafearn Forest, and from Coignafearn
Lodge to the nearest house (Stronelarig Lodge on
the head waters of Loch Killin) the distance is ten
miles as the crow flies. Between these two lodges
lies a wilderness of desolate mountains just under
the 3,000 contour-line.

I did not penetrate to Dalbeg. Charles St.
John, the naturalist, gives us an account of the
sport he enjoyed when at Coignafearn and the
summer shieling of Dalbeg in 1847.

The morning was bright . . . every little pool was
dimpled by the rising trout. . . . Beautiful in its grand
and wild solitude is the glen where the Findhorn takes
its rise. It is too remote even for the sportsman, and the
grouse cock crows in peace, and struts without fear of
pointer or gun when he comes down from the hill slopes
at noon-day to sip the clear waters of the springs that give
birth to this beautiful river. The red deer fearlessly quenches
his thirst in them. . . . Seldom is he annoyed by the
presence of mankind unless a chance shepherd or poacher
from Badenoch happens to wander in that direction.

M

Having read the above extract, it is interesting to note that in 1908 the Coignafearn bag was 4,832½ brace of grouse and 37 stags.

The main sources of the Findhorn are the two streams, the Eskin and the Amhuinn Cro Clach. Here, among these desolate mountains, there are occasional water spouts and cloudbursts, and these have been the means of the sudden and devastating floods for which the Findhorn has always been notorious. In its lower reaches a mighty volume of water has sometimes thundered down its channel with a solid front like a tidal wave.

There are five very old holdings in this upper region, each of which goes by the name of *Coig*, which means "a fifth"—Coignascalen, Coigna-finternach, Coignashee, Coignavullin, and Coigna-fearn. These are the five "fifths" of Strath-dearn. In ancient times in Ireland a *coig* or fifth meant a fairly large province. Hence the old Gaelic proverb, "Better is one-fifth in Ireland than the five-fifths of Strathdearn." In this valley of the Coigs the scenery is wild and rather desolate, but when you come down to Glen Mazeran and Glen Kyllachy, you are in the region of trees and green pastures. To all pedestrians I would recommend a delightful hill walk of seven or eight miles up Glen Kyllachy and over

THE FINDHORN BELOW THE STREENS (NEAR DRYNACHAN)

[To face page 170

the Caochan Breac, a fine 1,500 foot pass which takes you across the hills and down to Farr, in Strathnairn.

I lingered more than once at the old church of Dalarossie, which stands on a green knoll above a delightful pool. This very small church has been restored, and tradition says that it stands on the site of an ancient Columban settlement. Some maintain that it was dedicated to St. Fergus in the eighth century, but this is doubtful. An old stone font lies in the grass of the churchyard. There are several uncanny stories about Dalarossie Church. One is that it is haunted, and that a certain skull disappears regularly and comes back again mysteriously. Another is that the Druids long ago sifted the soil of this sacred spot so carefully that for ten feet down no stones or pebbles are found. But this may only be a compliment to the Celtic monks who cultivated their beautiful precincts to perfection.

The memorials, although not ancient, tell of the gentles and simples who from time immemorial have been buried here—a Lord of Session who loved the place so well that his name is carved on the restored church; a weaver of Balvraid who died in 1830; a Chief Clerk of the House of Lords; a schoolmaster, shepherds, shoemakers, tacksmen, and farmers. The schoolmaster taught in the united parishes for sixty years and died at the age of ninety.

All about Tomatin there are green pastures with pine trees and some of the finest moors in Scotland. Through this pleasant land the river meanders in broad sweeps right down to the beginning of The Streens. The by-road which leaves the Great North Road between Tomatin and Loch Moy passes down the open valley of the Findhorn past Ruthven and then through natural birch woods and junipers until it comes to an end at Pollochaig— now, alas, an empty and derelict farm house.

Nearby there is a Bucket Bridge. A square wooden "bucket" seated for four persons runs on wire ropes from one side of the river to the other. It is worked by a large wheel-and-handle arrangement from either bank. Being alone, I could not sit in the bucket and "caw" myself over by working the handle from the bank. So I took all risks and sat down in the bucket which ran down the sagging ropes until it reached midstream. There, naturally, it stopped. I had then to pull myself and the bucket up the incline by means of a middle wire rope across the bucket, and it took all my pith to pull home. Otherwise, I might have been sitting long enough above the river in that solitary spot. The return journey was all the more of an adventure because of the added apprehension of an elderly and solid man. The next time I use the Bucket Bridge I shall oil the rusty wheels.

Having crossed the bridge I walked down the right bank of the river and through part of the Pass of Pollochaig which is called The Streens. Here the river tumbles between steep crags and screes for about four miles. The place names are interesting. Findhorn was originally *Fionn-eireann*, literally " White Ireland," which doubtless referred to the great expanse of dazzling sands at the mouth of the estuary. There is near Dulsie Bridge to-day a large fort called Dunearn, or Ireland's Fort, indicating that the district of White Ireland stretched far inland. Indeed, the old name of Strathdearn, or *Srath-eireann*, applied to the even remoter district of the Coigs already mentioned. The Streens, on the other hand, is Struan or *Sruthan*, " the stream place," an exact description of the four miles of turbulent water rushing between the steep screes from Pollochaig to Drynachan.

The geology of The Streens is of great interest. This Pass of Pollochaig was not always the natural outlet of the River Findhorn. A great lake, or series of lakes, must have filled the valley above

The Streens at one time. You can see the old
terraces all up and down the river above Pollochaig, and they point to a great body of still
water. The Findhorn at one time must have struck
off by way of the Funtack Burn, then through
Loch Moy, and so into the valley of the River
Nairn. But a gap in the great barrier at Pollochaig was gradually worn through, and the
water then carved out the narrow gorge of The
Streens. The outfall was then drawn away from
Loch Moy, and rushed through the new channel
at Pollochaig, and so to the sea.

Near Pollochaig stands the Hill of Treasure, an
island before the great lake burst through the
barrier. The hill is so-called because somewhere
on it the Mackintoshes buried their treasures when
the Cummings were expected to raid Moy Hall.
Again, on the right bank of the river there is the
Hill of Parting. Here local tradition tells us that
the Earl of Mar took leave of his friend Ewan
Cameron and five of his faithful followers after
the battle of Inverlochy. Yet again, on the steep
and rocky left bank of the river there is a beetling
crag where a golden eagle used to build its eyrie.
For hundreds of years the Macqueens occupied
Pollochaig. Indeed, I counted many Macqueen
tombstones in the churchyard of Moy. It was a

Macqueen who slew the last wolf in this district in 1743. Wolves lingered in the Monadh Liath longer than in any other part of the Highlands.

I was very anxious to explore the river as far as Glenferness. I was taken down the famous Rock Walk by the river, and I was also guided to the Princess Stone. For, unless you actually walk through The Streens to Drynachan Lodge, and then down the river to Dulsie Bridge (which is a good ten-mile walk) you must approach Glenferness either by a long motor circuit by Daviot and Cawder on the north side, or by Carr Bridge and the Lochindorb moor road on the south. Both are beautiful. At Dulsie Bridge there is a fine view both up and down the river gorge, with its deep black pools and foaming falls, where on the quiet evenings you can watch the salmon leaping.

Glenferness is such a beautiful place that I do not doubt the local story about the Lord Leven and Melville, who first purchased the estate. He sent in an offer. Then he went for a stroll down the Rock Walk. He returned immediately to the house, and dispatched an amended offer, which increased the first by several thousands of pounds. The whole place is a paradise of trees; the river gorge is one of the very finest on the Findhorn; and the moors stretch away beyond the woodlands.

The mansion-house stands on an eminence above the river, with a stretch of level lawns in front, and a magnificent view down the river from the back windows. The Rock Walk takes you right down the side of the ravine, being partly built against the cliff, with a striking view of all the pools, falls, and cataracts. When Jenny Lind was a visitor at Glenferness the sight of the river from the Rock Walk made her burst into song. To walk down this path during a spate must be a terrifying experience, for the water literally roars through the defile. I remarked that there was surely a rumble of thunder. But my guide smiled and told me that it was only the sound of moving boulders in the deep pools. What then must the sound be like when a spate is on !

My chief desire was to see the Princess Stone, to which I was led through a thicket of great trees by the river-side. It is a grey stone, hoary with age, elaborately carved on both sides, with Celtic circles and interlacings, many mysterious symbols like the spectacle ornament, the sceptre, the crescent, the V-shaped ornament, curious animals, a panel at the foot with two figures embracing each other, and on the broken top the remains of a Celtic cross greatly defaced.

A thousand years ago, as the old legend tells

us, the Raven of Denmark took his dark flight over
Moray's fair fields.   The Scots were no match for
the sea rovers.   But a King of Scots who lived
at Lochindorb Castle gathered a great army of
Highlanders and defeated the Vikings.   Among
the prisoners taken was a son of the Danish King,
and he was put in the dungeon at Lochindorb.
When the Royal Dane heard of the defeat of his
men and the capture of his son, he sent messengers
to the King of Scots and concluded a treaty, one
part of which was that the Danish Prince should
marry the Scots Princess.   The King of Scots
saw the advantage of the treaty ; and it was sealed
by both Kings.

Meantime the Princess in her bower and the
Prince in his dungeon had fallen deeply in love with
one another, all unconscious of the happy con-
tract.   With the help of a servant they arranged
an elopement.   One dark night they stole out of
the island castle, entered a boat, and landed on
the north side of the loch.   There, a fleet horse was
waiting, and the Prince, lifting the Princess on to
the saddle behind him, rode off to the Findhorn
valley.   At Dulsie they found the river in flood,
and dismounted to win a better crossing when the
water subsided.   But when the dawn light came
they saw pursuers on the height above them,

among whom was the Scots King himself. The Princess, alarmed at the thought of her father's interference, urged the Prince to risk the river. So they plunged into the swollen flood, horse and all, while the frantic father cried after them the good news which they could not hear for the roar of the river. Torn from the saddle, the lovers appeared on the surface for a moment, and then disappeared in the torrent. Their bodies were found lying on a grassy bank, and on the same spot the King raised the beautifully carved memorial, which to this day is called the Princess Stone.

XX

THE FINEST RIVER IN SCOTLAND :
II—THE LOWER FINDHORN

WHEN first I learned that the great naturalist, Charles St. John, and Benjamin Jowett, the famous Master of Balliol, had both called the Findhorn River the most beautiful in Britain, I rather suspected that, like all generalisations, this was a gross exaggeration. I did not know the river then. But now that I have explored it for myself, I have slowly but surely come to the same conclusion.

There is an old Moray proverb, which says : " Speak weel o' the hielan's, but live in the laich." I do not wonder that some Moray loon coined that saying. A great and a goodly land, washed by the northern sea, and arched over by infinite skies. Indeed, so great is the variety of scenery along its banks that the Findhorn is not one river, but many. Having already explored from the wilds of Coignafearn to Glenferness, I returned to explore the lower reaches, which even surpass the upper.

I never lean over Dulsie Bridge to gaze at the wooded gorge but I think of Robert Burns. In

1787, Burns passed this way, and stayed at Dulsie, where there was an inn. But the supreme passionist of the human heart had little eye for scenery, apart from the fact that it reminded him of some aspect of human life. *Afton Water* only reminded him of his Mary asleep by the murmuring stream. In his immortal *Banks and Braes o' Bonnie Doon* the warbling birds, the rose, the woodbine, and the flowering thorn all reminded the broken-hearted lover of joys departed, never to return. So we are not surprised, that his Diary was woefully matter-of-fact when he was at Dulsie and the Findhorn.

" *Monday* (*3rd Sept.*), enter Strathspey—come to Sir James Grant's—dine—company—Lady Grant a sweet, pleasant body—Mr. and Miss Bailie, Mrs. Bailie, Dr. and Mrs. Grant—clergymen—Mr. Hepburn—come through mist and darkness to Dulsie to lie.

" *Tuesday* (*4th Sept.*), Findhorn River—rocky banks——"

But, at Castle Grant, the lovely Miss Leslie Bailie made such an impression on the poet that she became the Bonny Lesley of one of his later songs.

Below Glenferness a side road leads you down to an ancient haunt of peace—Ardclach, with its Bell Tower on the hill and its Church down in the hollow by the river.

The ancient square Bell Tower stands on the

summit of a bracken-covered hill, commanding a fine view over the countryside. Two hundred and fifty feet below it, in the sheltered dell by the river, stands the parish kirk among its graves. As you climb up to the tower, you get glimpses of a white manse, surrounded by well-kept lawns, and a flower-garden, an ideal place of rest. On the tower itself, there is the date 1655, marking the year when it was rebuilt. Long ago it was used as a watch tower, from which an alarm could be given to the whole countryside when the wild Highland raiders swept down Strathdearn. The upper chamber was for the watchman, who lived there in comfort, with a fireplace, a garderobe recess in the wall, and three single-paned lights. The lower chamber was the prison. The bell was used both for calling the country people to church, and for giving alarm in time of raids. It is said that on one occasion the raiders threw a particularly fine bell into the river, where there is a deep pool. Many attempts were made to find it, but all in vain; and some say that when a great spate is on, the sound of the bell can be heard as it is rolled about on the floor of the pool by the surging torrent.

When that human nightingale, Jenny Lind, was staying at Glenferness, the rural postman at Belivat

was also the precentor in the Kirk of Ardclach.
When he was delivering letters on the Saturday
morning, old Lord Leven invited him into the
drawing-room to hear Jenny Lind sing. The postman, of course, was enchanted, and with a delightful
naïveté told Jenny Lind that he was a singer himself !

"I am the precentor in the Parish Kirk of Ardclach," said he.

"Then," replied the great singer, "because you
have honoured me by coming to hear me sing to-
day, I shall come to church to hear you sing
to-morrow."

Next day, the precentor pitched the tune too
high, because of the excitement of the occasion.
The congregation did not usually join in until the
first line was sung, but Jenny Lind did, and the
psalm became such a fine duet that no one else
dared sing for listening. Before the end, even the
precentor stopped singing that he might listen
to the most wonderful rendering of the psalm as
a solo that any one in Scotland has probably ever
heard.

The reason why the Bell Tower was built on the
highest hill was that every one might hear the bell,
and the reason why the church was built on the
very water's edge was that all who dwell on the

other side of the river might have easy access (across a bridge) to the sanctuary.

The road from Dava Station sweeps down and across the Findhorn at Logie Bridge, a little below Ardclach; but this Logie must not be confused with the beautiful House of Logie that lies below Relugas. As you cross this bridge and climb the road to Belivat, you get a magnificent view from the monument hill of the winding river and its wooded banks—a wide and peaceful view which gives you the impression that the river is resting for a mile or two between its upper and lower gorges.

Between this and the next bridge at Daltulich, the road once more leaves the river, which can only be seen here by walking through the beautiful grounds of Coulmony. Here is an utterly quiet and remote stretch of the Findhorn. The house stands far above the river, with a garden and a sloping lawn ablaze with beds of flowers. The river path below the house follows the water's edge all the way down to the bridge, and the black pool below Coulmony is one of the finest bits of water on the river.

Henry Mackenzie, *The Man of Feeling*, was a cousin of the laird of Coulmony-Rose of Kilravock and he often stayed at this beautiful retreat. At that time the laird was planting trees, making walks,

and improving the whole property. Henry Mackenzie, however, showed how insensate " The
Man of Feeling " could be, for he wrote to his
cousin, " How do your walks and plantations go
on ? If I were with you I should be apt to plant
stones merely to write inscriptions on them." He
actually sent some doggerel verses to be placed on
trees and stones about Coulmony for the delecta-
tion of visitors to that lovely spot. For the river-
side walk, he composed an " Ode to Melancholy " ;
for the approach to the grounds, an " Ode to Pity " ;
and for the public in general, this doubtful sentiment, " The stranger's steps are welcome here."
Needless to say the learned laird rejected all those
insults to the scenery.

Daltulich Bridge, a single arch of granite, reminds
me of an excellent story about the local contractor
who built it. The first bridge he built on the
spot collapsed when it was finished, so the contractor had to erect a second on the spot, and at
his own expense. When a friend condoled with
him on having to bear the double cost, he replied
quite cheerily, " It micht hae been waur, gin I hadna
estimated eneuch to gie me a profit on twa brigs."

From Daltulich Bridge, right down by Relugas
and Logie to Sluie, is the most beautiful and
romantic stretch of the Findhorn. The combination

THE FINDHORN GORGE, NEAR FERNESS

[*To face page* 184]

of rocky gorges, magnificent woodlands, and turbulent waters, which thunder between great cliffs and tumble over wild boulders, is unsurpassed by any river scenery in Scotland.

The road crosses Daltulich Bridge and joins the main road on the right bank of the river, hiding it from view for about a mile. Then come the glories of Relugas.

Relugas House stands on a rocky height between the gorge of the river Divie and the gorge of the Findhorn. Here is the poet's dream of a hermitage —the old yellow harled house, now empty, with a huddle of homely gables and chimneys and quaint windows, perched on its beetling crag above the wild waters. There is a sweep of lawns and great trees about the house; an old grey stone-balus-traded stair descends from the house to the gardens, which are beautifully kept. They lie in a pocket of sunshine above the river, and on this September day they were blazing with colour. There was no one there to break the thrum of peace as we wandered about the sandy walks, listening to the rush of the river, and hemmed in on every side by great trees that seem to brood in the heat. Again and again my eyes rested on that grey stair of romance, all lichened with age, a reminder of the old days when Sir Thomas Dick Lauder lived

N

here during the great flood of 1829. The pathway down the Divie gorge is wild in the extreme. If you follow it right down, you will come to the junction of the Divie and the Findhorn—a most romantic spot—and so return up the Findhorn to Randolph's Leap. There are two intensely interesting Flood Mark Stones—one above the meeting of the waters, which has the following inscription on it, " *Findhorn and Divie met here in flood, Augt. 3rd and 4th,* 1829 "; the other, above Randolph's Leap, with this inscription on it, " *Flood Mark, August 3rd and 4th,* 1829."

Standing above these stones on this quiet autumn day it is impossible to imagine that the waters rose so high. But of the facts are recorded by Sir Thomas Dick Lauder, in his now famous *Account of the Moray Floods of August,* 1829 :

At Randolph's Leap the rise was forty-six feet, flooding Rannoch Haugh, making a total rise of fifty feet above the ordinary level of the water. At the meeting of the waters, where the Divie and the Findhorn join, the waves tossed themselves twenty feet into the air. Climbing out on to the rocks of the little peninsula to-day, the waters seem fierce enough, but it is quite unthinkable what the conditions must have been like when these roaring floods met with a thirty-feet rise right above your head. The Relugas gardener caught a salmon with an umbrella, fifty feet above the ordinary level of the water, and here the stone marking this highest rise above Randolph's Leap stands to-day.

The original edition of the *Account* has remarkable little woodcuts, showing the vital flood points both before and after, and only those who examine these contemporary drawings, can have any idea of the terrific damage done by this historic flood. The sound of the waters must have been fearsome. As Sir Thomas Dick Lauder says : " The noise was a distinct combination of two kinds of sounds ; one, a uniformly continued roar, the other like rapidly repeated discharges of many cannons at once. The first of these proceeded from the violence of the water; the other, which was heard through it, and as it were, muffled by it, came from the enormous stones which the stream was hurling over its uneven bed of rocks."

The name of Randolph's Leap is a strange anomaly, for, as far as I can find out, Randolph did not leap the gorge, but was the means of making another man do it. Regent Randolph was hard pressing the Comyns in battle. The Comyns were rallied under Alistair Bane of Dunphail, who fought a desperate rearguard action through the woods, and continued the fight to

the Findhorn at Relugas. But, on the opposite
bank he found his enemies awaiting him. The
pressure on the rear pushed the desperate Comyns
nearer and nearer the chasm, until at last, in des-
peration, Alistair flung the standard of the Comyns
across the gorge among his enemies, leapt after
it, crying, " Let the bravest keep it ! "—and so
he actually cut his way to safety through his enemies.
This gorge, therefore, should be called Comyns'
Leap.

Logie House, as the name indicates, stands
above a " hollow." It is a fine old Scots mansion-
house, beautifully restored by Sir Alexander Grant
of Logie, Relugas, and Dunphail. Here again
there is a lovely riverside walk, below which
there are some long, black pools in the gorge.
There was a Celtic cell in the haugh below Logie.
It is mentioned in the old Roman Catholic records
of Moray, but there are no traces of it to-day.
Between Logie and Sluie there are some famous
esses, or waterfalls (Gaelic, *eas*), pot-holes, whirlpools, and rapids, and then comes Sluie pool, a
long, calm sheet of water.

It was at Logie House that the Sobieskie Stuart
brothers, who claimed descent from Prince Charlie,
stayed in the year of the Great Flood. They were
keen sportsmen, and have left behind them a delight-

ful proof of that in their " Lays of the Deer Forest."
The Earl of Moray gave them permission to fish
and shoot on his side of the river, and allowed
them to build a little hut for their use. It was
built, says Charles, the younger brother, " on a
high and beautiful craig at the crook of the river
near the Little Ess—a precipice eighty feet in height
. . . a little cell large enough to hold two beds,
a bench, a hearth, a table, and a kistie." There
the Sobieskie Stuarts spent many happy days and
nights " when the storm rent the pines above,
and the roaring thunder of the river came down
below."

The " Bonny Lesley " of Robert Burns married Robert Cumming of Logie, and, as so often
happens, this most beautiful lady married a man
who was particularly plain looking. Indeed, his
relative, Mrs. Smith of Baltiboys, describes him as
" a fine, tall-looking man, with a very ugly Scots
face, sandy hair, and huge mouth, ungainly man yet
kindly, very simple in character—in short, a kind
of goose." However, the lovely lady of Logie
had that supreme art of womanhood—she managed
her husband and everybody else at Logie without
letting it appear that she was doing it.

Of the final flanks of Findhorn—the great
estates of Darnaway on the left bank, and Altyre

on the right bank—I will only say that the Earls
of Moray at Darnaway and the Cummings of
Altyre made history in Scotland for many
centuries. The Kings of Scotland passed through
Darnaway, and the Cummings of Altyre were
settled on their estate when the Red Comyn was
stabbed in the Greyfriars Kirk at Dumfries by
Robert the Burce in 1305. An old laird of Altyre
was once asked, " To whom does the Darnaway
land on the other side of the river belong ? " His
answer was, " To the Earl of Moray—but, the views
are mine."

So might it be said of the Findhorn River
to-day—the views belong to every man.

XXI

BYWAYS OF KINCARDINE : GLENBERVIE AND DUNNOTTAR

HE who travels only on main roads seldom sees the real countryside, and certainly never comes upon the ancient haunts of peace. So in the quiet days of September I explored many of the cross-roads and byways of Kincardineshire, and came on many of the beauty spots which are tucked away in corners of that land which lies to the south of the Royal Dee.

One of these was Glenbervie. You will find it to the west of the great Aberdeen road near a little village called Drumlithie. The real object of my journey was Glenbervie churchyard, so I naturally thought of Glenbervie Kirk. But I found the church on the roadside without a single grave round it—a rather bald, modern building, with no sense of sanctuary about it such as graves and old trees supply. After some inquiries I found that the old churchyard of Glenbervie is reached by going down a side lane. There, among

umbrageous trees, stands the old manse of Glenbervie, and behind it the ancient kirkyard, with
the grounds of Glenbervie House just across the
Bervie Water. The whole place is buried in
immemorial trees, and the churchyard is not only
old, but of great extent.

In the centre of the churchyard stand two massive flat gravestones, each supported on four little
stone pillars. Beneath these stones lie buried the
great-grandparents and the great-grand-uncle of our
national poet, Robert Burns—only the Glenbervie
name was always spelled Burness. This great-
grandfather of Burns was a shoemaker at Stenhouse
of Mergie, near Rickarton; but he afterwards
rented the lonely farm of Bogjorgan.

Robert Burns visited the district of Stonehaven
in 1787, being naturally drawn to it because his
own father had left the farm of Clochnahill and
settled in Ayrshire. The poet spent two days
among his relatives in the paternal country, and
wrote to his brother that he "found our aunts
Jean and Isabel still alive."

The day I visited his ancestral graves was lown
and still. The Bervie Water whispered down the
little glen. The great trees stood motionless, as
if in a reverie of reminiscence, and an atmosphere
of bygone days seemed to brood over the whole

place. Instinctively I trod softly among the graves in the utter solitude. Little did those hard-working farmers, the great-grandfather and the great-grand-uncle of the poet, know that long after they had become dust in Glenbervie pilgrims would come here to search for their tombstones out of rever-ance for their illustrious descendant.

But I was yet to come on another unexpected link with the little farm of Bogjorgan and the William and James of the Glenbervie stones. The very next Sunday afternoon I walked out to Dunnottar Church and churchyard. It was appro-priate that when I had previously visited the grim ruin of Dunnottar Castle the day was dark and lowering, the sea grey, and the ruin shrouded in gloom. But, just as appropriately, when I walked out to Dunnottar Kirk it was a warm, sunny afternoon. Much of the right seeing of a place depends upon the atmosphere of the day.

The road from Stonehaven to Dunnottar Kirk is one of great beauty, the trees arching overhead and forming an avenue of delicious shade by the side of the Carron Water. Then a little road to the right, and there, fornent you, stand the kirk, the kirkyard and the manse, all perched on a mound above the stream. Close by is the Witches' Pool,

the scene of many a cruel drowning in the old unhappy days when a woman with a gift of divining
was taken for a witch.   As at Glenbervie, there are
plenty of trees near the kirk and manse of Dunnottar
—but, unlike Glenbervie, the whole place beaks in
the sun on a slope that is open to all the light of
heaven.   The God's acre is kept to perfection.

Here, by the path, stands the stone-slated burial
vault of the Keith Marischals of Dunnottar.   The
" G.K.M.—1852 " refers to the builder, George
Keith, fifth Earl Marischal, founder of Marischal
College in Aberdeen.   In 1913 this vault was
restored in grateful memory by the University of
Aberdeen.   But the money which George Keith
gave to Aberdeen was said by some to have been
stolen from the Church.   The Marischal made
the sturdy reply which is now the famous motto
of the family.   It is carved above the inner door
of the Mitchell Hall at Marischal College : Thay
Haif Said.   Quhat Say Thay ?   Lat Thame Say.

Wandering about among the native graves, I
noticed a countryman examining a tombstone
with great interest.   I glanced at the name on the
stone, and found it was Burness.   " Is that the
same family of Burness which is on the stones
of Robert Burns's ancestors in Glenbervie Churchyard ? " I asked him.   " The very same," he

replied. " I am called Robert Burness, and these
are the graves of my ancestors." Here was one
who was actually akin to the poet! Then he
launched forth on the whole family history, for he
had the genealogy at his finger ends. These
Dunnottar stones mark the burial-place of the
descendants of William, the poet's great-grandfather, who is buried in Glenbervie.

The most famous stone in Dunnottar Kirkyard,
however, is the Covenanters' Stone, a plain upright slab, which is protected by an iron rim. Here
are preserved the names of some of the Covenanters
who died in Dunnottar Castle :

Here lyes John Stot, James Atchison, James Russell,
and William Broun, and one whose name wee have not
gotten, and two women whose names also wee know not ;
and two who perished comeing doune the rock ; one whose
name was James Watson, the other not known, who all
died prisoners in Dunnottar Castle, anno. 1685, for their
adherence to the word of God and Scotlands Covenanted
work of Reformation. Rev. xi. ch., 12 verse.

Here, for the first and only time, Sir Walter
Scott met Robert Paterson, that true-blue Covenanting mason and wandering inscription-cutter,
who went up and down the country kirkyards of
Scotland keeping fresh the inscriptions on the
martyr tombstones with his hammer and chisel.
As I stood by the stone on that September Sunday

afternoon, I seemed to hear the click of the chisel
on the stone, and to see the white pony of " Old
Mortality " nibbling a sweet morsel of grass close
by.

" Old Mortality " was a native of Hawick.
Scott gives us an unforgettable picture of him
which may be shortly summed up thus. The old
man wore a very large blue Kilmarnock bonnet
over his grey hair : had a hodden grey coat, with
waistcoat and breeches of the same homely cloth,
in decent repair but very old ; clouted hobnail
shoes ; black cloth leggings ; while alongside of
him in the kirkyard was a very old and hollow-
eyed white horse feeding among the graves. Scott
tried to get into conversation with this remarkable
man whom he was to immortalise. but Paterson
was very dour and dull, and in a bad humour
because, as Scott says, " his spirit had been sorely
vexed by hearing the psalmody directed by a pitch
pipe in some Aberdeen kirk, and he had no freedom
of conversation."

But to-day, even a true-blue Presbyterian and
lover of the Covenanters must never forget that
Episcopal clergymen at a later date, suffered
imprisonment for breaking a law which forbade
them preaching to more than four of their people
at a time. In those days all Episcopalians were

suspected of being Jacobites, and disloyal to King George.

For example, George Troup, the Episcopal minister of Muchalls, with his Episcopal brothers of Drumlithie and Stonehaven, was imprisoned in the old Tolbooth of Stonehaven in 1748 for six months. Troup carried a bagpipe with him on the way to prison, playing the Jacobite air, "O'er the Water to Charlie."

Yet during their imprisonment those Episcopal parsons baptised many children. The mothers at all risks concealed their children in creels which they carried on their backs, crossing the burn at the "Water Yett," and clambering across the rocks to the back door of the Tolbooth. There they waited their chance of getting to the cell of their clergyman, where the rite was performed.

There is a questionable tradition that Scott wrote a little bit of "Old Mortality" under a great elm tree on the lawn in front of Dunnottar manse. No elm tree is there now, but on the edge of the lawn, before the manse door, a round mound shows exactly where this large tree once stood. This tree was taken down because it was becoming dangerous to the manse, and two chairs for the Communion Table were made of the wood. These chairs now stand in the church.

So, in those two quiet places of graves I came on
Mortality and Immortality.   God's sunshine tem-
pered with an invisible breeze.   Fruit ripening in
the old manse garden, and little robins singing their
plaintive litanies in the silence.   Also, I had met in
spirit the two greatest Scotsmen who ever held a
pen—Robert Burns and Walter Scott.